AI Visibility Playbook

Governing the Signals That Shape Search, Reputation, and Digital Trust

Ash Nallawalla

https://www.linkedin.com/in/ashnallawalla

Keywords: AI, Artificial Intelligence, Web Content, Large Language Models (LLMs), Visibility Governance, Content Policy, Risk Management, Compliance, SEO Governance, semantic architecture

658.872 Technology and Application of Knowledge > Management and auxiliary services > Management > Of Marketing

BISAC:

- **BUS101000 BUSINESS & ECONOMICS / Consulting**
- BUS090050 BUSINESS & ECONOMICS / E-Commerce / Search Engine Optimization
- BUS104000 BUSINESS & ECONOMICS / Corporate Governance
- BUS043060 BUSINESS & ECONOMICS / Marketing / Digital

TABLE OF CONTENTS

PREFACE

In the past, visibility meant ranking high in search engine results. Today, it means **being selected and reused by AI systems** that interpret, summarize, and deliver information long before a user ever reaches your website. This is "AI Visibility, which we cover in Book 4, *Is Our SEO Working?*, but that requires solid governance foundations, covered in this book.

Platforms like Google now blend traditional search results with AI Overviews, AI Mode, and other generative surfaces that answer questions directly. These answers shape user decisions, often without a single click.

This shift has created a world of **zero-click customers**—people who compare products, understand services, and even complete transactions based on information extracted and synthesised by AI systems. When these systems lift material from your site, it is usually because you already have **strong SEO foundations**: clear structure, accurate metadata, consistent terminology, authoritative definitions, and predictable templates. In other words, content that performs well in AI-mediated search tends to have strong SEO. But SEO alone is not enough.

WHY "VISIBILITY GOVERNANCE"

Throughout this book, I use the term *Visibility Governance* rather than the broader, more common term *Digital Governance*. The distinction is deliberate. Digital governance describes the systems, platforms, and policies an organization operates. Visibility governance describes the outcome those systems now control: whether your organization is found, how it is represented, and what meaning is extracted and reused by search engines and AI systems.

In an AI-mediated environment, visibility increasingly occurs outside your owned digital properties—inside AI summaries, comparisons, and zero-click answers that shape decisions without a website visit. Governing "digital" infrastructure alone is no longer sufficient. What must be governed is visibility itself: the signals, structures, and controls that determine how your organization appears, or fails to appear, across human and machine-interpreted discovery surfaces.

For clarity, *Visibility Governance* sits within the broader discipline of digital governance, but it names the specific business risk and strategic outcome this book addresses.

Why Governance Is the Missing Link

Both forms of visibility—**traditional rankings and AI-generated answers**—depend on something deeper: **governance**. Policies, controls, workflow discipline, and clear ownership determine whether your material remains accurate, extractable, compliant, and safe to reuse across AI-driven surfaces. Governance protects visibility by ensuring the content that represents your organisation is consistent and trustworthy, no matter how platforms evolve.

This book shows you how to build that governance. It helps you create the structures that keep your organisation's meaning stable across websites, apps, AI summaries, and the discovery systems that shape digital reputation.

Over the past two decades, as I've advised organizations on SEO strategy, one truth has become impossible to ignore: **governance is the missing link**.

In the early years, websites were often built by a single enthusiastic employee—someone with vision, but little oversight. Today, digital operations have matured, and some governance has emerged. But SEO itself remains largely ungoverned: fragmented across departments, reactive in execution, and rarely aligned with enterprise risk or performance frameworks. **This book addresses that gap.**

Most corporations apply governance principles to their core functions—finance, risk, compliance, operations—because they understand the cost of unmanaged risk. But two domains now central to marketing—**websites and AI**—are still treated as creative playgrounds rather than operational assets. That's a governance blind spot.

AI tools are being used across the enterprise—by interns, analysts, and executives alike—often without policy, oversight, or accountability. Large Language Models (LLMs) ingest vast quantities of data, much of it scraped from websites without consent. This has already triggered litigation, which this book does not explore. But the implications are clear: **your web content is now part of the AI supply chain**, whether you intended it or not.

Some brands may benefit from this exposure—especially when users query LLMs for product comparisons or brand-specific insights. But without governance, those benefits are accidental. And the risks— reputational, legal, operational—are real.

Visibility governance can help.

HOW THIS BOOK IS USED

This book is used as preparatory material for the **Visibility Governance Maturity Workshop (VGMM)**. It establishes shared language, scope, and context before the workshop, ensuring participants approach governance questions from a common baseline. The workshop itself is a facilitated executive session that produces a current-state governance determination; this book supports that process but does not replace the workshop or function as an assessment, audit, or scoring tool.

HOW THIS BOOK FITS INTO THE SERIES

This is the third volume in the *Managing SEO* series. It focuses on extending corporate governance principles into the digital and AI environments that now define marketing operations. The book establishes frameworks for AI policy, ethical data use, and interdepartmental accountability across marketing, legal, and technical teams.

- ***Book 1, Managing SEO,*** serves as a concise strategic overview for busy managers, unifying the themes of the series without duplicating the detailed material covered in each book.
- ***Book 2, Accidental SEO Manager,*** equips managers with the operational basics of running SEO programs and managing agencies.
- ***Book 4, Is Our SEO Working?*** Turns governance principles into measurable performance—showing how to evaluate SEO outcomes and maintain continuous improvement. It goes deeper into AI Visibility.
- ***Book 5, The C-suite Blind Spot,*** brings governance and measurement together at the executive level, guiding leadership in aligning SEO with corporate performance and fiduciary oversight.

– Melbourne, February 2026

Chapter 1

THE AI-MEDIATED SEARCH LANDSCAPE

THE AI-MEDIATED SEARCH LANDSCAPE

AI-mediated discovery now sits between your audience and your website. Google's AI Overviews and AI Mode, along with similar generative surfaces across other platforms, extract and synthesize information before a click ever happens. In many cases, users form opinions, evaluate options, and make decisions without ever visiting the source.

The material these systems select tends to reflect strong fundamentals rather than tactical optimization: clear structure, consistent terminology, authoritative definitions, accessible templates, and stable content patterns. These are not ranking tricks. They are signals that allow external systems to interpret, summarize, and reuse meaning safely.

This shift changes the nature of visibility. Discovery is no longer limited to ranked lists of links. It increasingly occurs inside synthesized answers, summaries, comparisons, and recommendations generated by machines that decide what to present and what to omit.

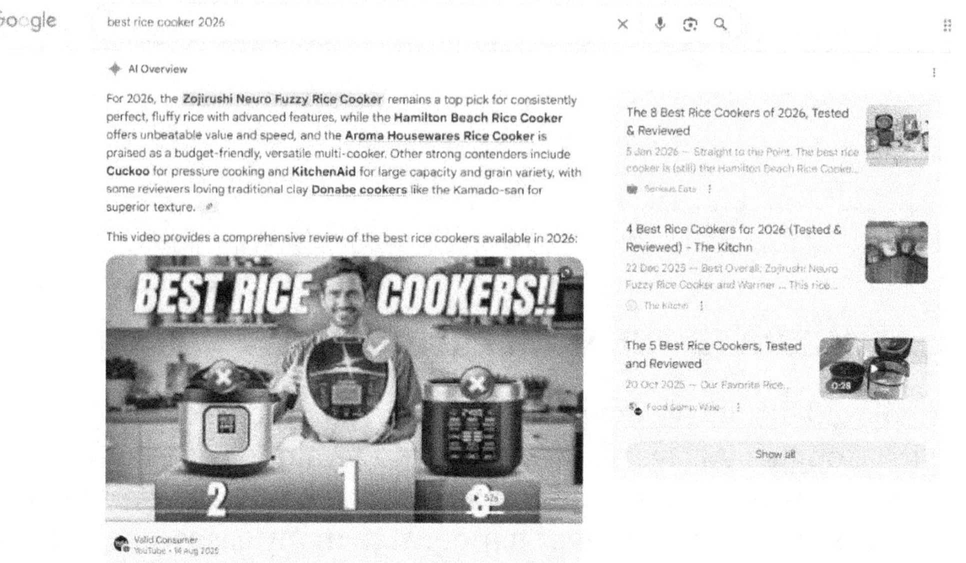

Figure 1 Google AI Overview can provide an answer without the user needing to click through.

VISIBILITY AND GOVERNANCE

Sustaining visibility in this environment requires something deeper than SEO tactics. It requires governance.

In an AI-mediated landscape, governance is not about controlling external systems. It is about ensuring that what your organization publishes is coherent, attributable, and interpretable when extracted and recombined outside your control.

This book focuses on visibility governance: the policies, ownership models, and workflows that maintain meaning stability as it moves from internal creation to external machine interpretation. Governance determines whether your content remains eligible for reuse when discovery happens through synthesis rather than clicks.

Before introducing the Visibility Governance Maturity Model (VGMM), it is necessary to clarify what governance means in this context and how it differs from operational execution or technology management.

What Governance Means in a Visibility Context

Governance defines who makes decisions, who carries responsibility, and how accountability is enforced. It turns informal judgment into a documented authority and a repeatable process.

In a visibility context, governance ensures that definitions remain consistent, ownership is explicit, review standards are applied predictably, and changes are traceable. It replaces dependence on individual expertise with institutional reliability that survives growth, turnover, and tooling changes.

Governance does not optimize content. It determines whether optimization can be trusted to scale without introducing ambiguity or risk.

AI-MEDIATED VISIBILITY AS A DISCOVERY SURFACE

AI-mediated systems do not simply retrieve information. They reconstruct meaning. They extract definitions, identify attributes, infer relationships, and reorganize material to match user intent.

Figure 2 The first organic ranking site is more than halfway down the page.

These systems operate on signals your organization publishes: headings, summaries, metadata, structured data, internal relationships, and consistency of terminology across assets. When those signals align, interpretation is reliable. When they conflict, systems deprioritize or exclude the source in favor of alternatives that present less risk.

How AI Discovery Systems Assemble Meaning

External systems favor material that behaves **predictably**. Definitions appear in expected locations. Attributes are grouped logically. Terminology remains stable across pages and formats. Relationships between concepts are reinforced rather than contradicted.

Governance enforces these conditions upstream. Without governance, signals drift as teams publish independently, adopt new tools, or update content unevenly. External systems interpret this drift as uncertainty and reduce reuse accordingly.

Retrieval, Re-Ranking, and Citation Selection

AI-mediated visibility depends less on generation than on retrieval. Before a response is synthesized, large language models that use retrieval-augmented generation transform a user's question into multiple internal queries ("fan-out" in Figure 4), retrieve candidate documents, and then re-rank those candidates before any text is generated. This retrieval phase determines which sources are even eligible to influence the final answer.

Query transformation is a critical but often invisible step. A single user question may be expanded into direct factual queries, contextual or temporal queries, verification-oriented queries, and entity-disambiguation queries. Each query retrieves a different candidate set, which is then merged and filtered. Content that is not retrievable across these variations is unlikely to appear consistently in AI-generated responses.

Re-ranking further narrows eligibility. Retrieved candidates are scored for relevance, clarity, entity alignment, and interpretive safety before generation begins. This means that optimization for AI visibility is fundamentally a retrieval problem first and a language problem second. Generation cannot compensate for weak retrieval signals.

Citation attachment, where it occurs, is a downstream effect of this process. Citations are not assigned to the "best" content in an abstract sense, but to content that supports specific claims during synthesis. As a result, being retrievable does not guarantee being cited, and being cited does not guarantee consistent inclusion across similar queries.

Some industry sources describe these behaviors as "Answer Engine Optimization" or "Generative Engine Optimization." While such labels can be heuristically useful, they do not describe new mechanisms. They reflect differing emphases within the same retrieval-driven system. From a governance perspective, the underlying requirement remains unchanged: content must be accessible, unambiguous, structurally coherent, and aligned to the entities and questions external systems are attempting to resolve.

The Role of Structured Content

Structured content plays an outsized role in AI-mediated discovery. Templates, semantic hierarchy, and consistent placement of key information allow systems to extract meaning without speculation.

Structure is not cosmetic. It determines whether a model can safely reuse your material. Governance preserves these structures through templates, review cycles, and ownership models that prevent fragmentation.

AI Overviews, AI Mode, and Interpretive Risk

AI Overviews and AI Mode illustrate how visibility now operates independently of traffic. A user may evaluate an organization entirely within these surfaces, forming conclusions without ever visiting the website.

When your material is selected, it reflects visibility governance maturity. When it is excluded, the cause is often ambiguity, inconsistency, or unresolved contradiction rather than a lack of optimization effort.

Figure 3 A user who invokes Google AI Mode is shown brands selected by an AI system.

UNDERSTANDING ZERO-CLICK VISIBILITY

Zero-click behavior is no longer an edge case. It is a core feature of AI-mediated discovery. Users obtain answers, comparisons, and recommendations directly from synthesized responses and move on without generating measurable sessions.

This creates an attribution gap. Influence occurs upstream, but traditional analytics fail to capture it. Governance provides stability by ensuring that content remains eligible for reuse even when engagement happens outside your environment.

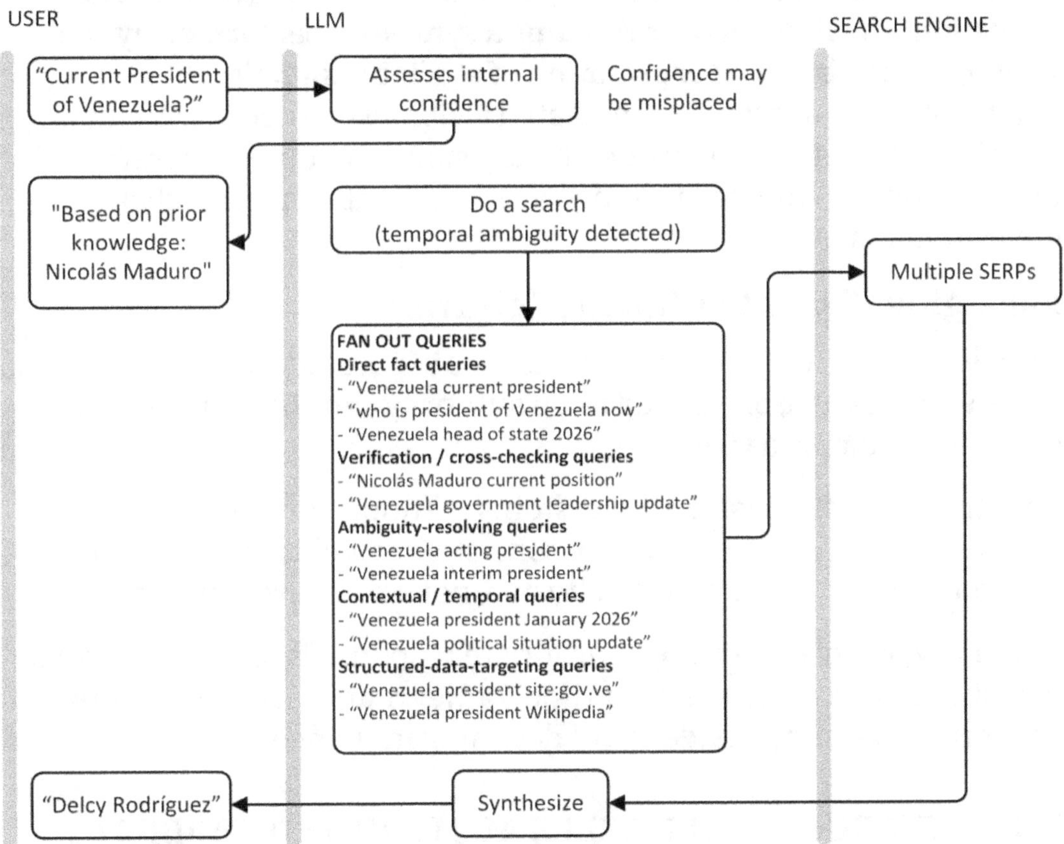

Figure 4 Example of AI-Mediated Question Handling With Conditional Web Grounding

This diagram (drawn in January 2026) illustrates how a large language model may respond to a factual query by first assessing its internal confidence, then deciding whether to retrieve external search results, before generating an answer. When internal confidence is deemed sufficient, the model may respond based solely on prior knowledge, which can reflect outdated or incomplete information. When uncertainty, temporal ambiguity, or conflicting signals are detected, the model may issue multiple search queries, retrieve results from search engines, and synthesize an answer from those inputs.

The sequence represents **process flow**, not verification, authority, or truth assurance. External search systems provide source material, not validation. **The final answer remains a synthesis performed by the model, shaped by its interpretation of available signals.** This distinction explains why AI-mediated visibility can occur without a website visit and why inclusion or exclusion from upstream retrieval directly affects how organizations are represented in zero-click environments.

Managing Visibility Without Referrals

In an executive context, visibility must be separated from traffic. Being cited, summarized, or implied as an authority can shape decisions without producing a visit.

The strategic risk is not that AI systems mention your organization without attribution. It is that they consistently mention competitors instead. This represents a visibility gap, not a measurement error.

At the governance level, the appropriate response is to track patterns of inclusion and exclusion over time, rather than treating declining sessions as definitive evidence of declining influence.

WHY GOVERNANCE ENABLES AI-MEDIATED VISIBILITY

Governance is a **visibility infrastructure**. It ensures that definitions, terminology, hierarchy, and attribution remain stable across assets and over time.

External systems prefer sources that reduce interpretive risk. When governance enforces consistency, it increases eligibility for reuse. When governance is weak, optimization becomes cosmetic and insufficient to influence synthesis-based discovery.

Governance also prevents amplification of weakness. Increased visibility does not correct underlying issues. It scales them. Without clear ownership and quality control, greater exposure accelerates reputational damage rather than preventing it.

VISIBILITY ASSETS AND BUSINESS INTENT

Every visibility asset requires explicit search intent. Websites, documentation hubs, product portals, and externally governed platforms all participate in discovery and trust formation, yet they are often managed in isolation.

Without a clear articulation of purpose, audience, and success criteria, governance becomes procedural rather than directional. Teams may follow standards without understanding trade-offs or escalation priorities.

The Visibility Governance Committee maintains asset-level intent, ensuring alignment with enterprise strategy and guiding prioritization decisions. This prevents optimization in isolation and anchors visibility work to long-term value.

CHARACTERISTICS OF EFFECTIVE VISIBILITY GOVERNANCE

Effective governance exhibits consistent traits that support trust, resilience, and interpretability.

Accountability and Ownership

Every decision and outcome has a **named owner**. This prevents
orphaned problems and ensures corrective action is driven rather than
assumed.

Transparency

Decision logic, review standards, and performance indicators are
visible and traceable through shared documentation. Transparency
builds confidence with stakeholders and reduces interpretive risk.

Compliance and Integrity

Legal obligations are met, but integrity extends beyond minimum
requirements. Decisions remain principled even where regulation is
silent, reducing downstream reputational exposure.

Responsiveness

Governance adapts to change. Early recognition of drift, dependency
failures, or interpretive risk prevents escalation.

Effectiveness and Efficiency

Governance supports delivery rather than obstructing it. It channels
effort toward outcomes that preserve meaning and trust.

Equity and Inclusiveness

Inclusive governance supports accessibility and fairness, improving
interpretability for both users and machines.

Participation and Collaboration

Cross-functional participation reduces blind spots and aligns content,
technical, legal, and operational perspectives.

Strategic Vision

Short-term decisions align with long-term visibility outcomes. Governance anticipates how exposure amplifies strengths and weaknesses.

Sustainability

Governance persists beyond individuals. It becomes institutional behavior rather than personal memory.

INTRODUCING THE VISIBILITY GOVERNANCE MATURITY MODEL (VGMM)

The Visibility Governance Maturity Model is the executive framework that unifies visibility oversight across domains.

VGMM is not an independent scoring system applied in isolation. It is a **derived maturity scale**, synthesized from operational maturity observed across its component domains. Content governance, SEO governance, website performance governance, accessibility, analytics, and related disciplines that feed upward into a consolidated visibility view.

VGMM exists to answer a fundamental question: whether the organization's internal discipline is sufficient to support reliable external interpretation at scale.

How VGMM Works

VGMM works by consolidating governance maturity across the domains that directly influence how meaning is created, maintained, and interpreted. These domains include content governance, SEO governance, website performance governance, accessibility governance, analytics reliability, and related operational disciplines that shape the signals published. Each domain is assessed independently, using observable practices rather than intent, and reflects how consistently that part of the organization produces interpretable, low-risk outputs.

The model's logic is additive rather than substitutive. Strength in one domain does not compensate for weakness in another. An organization with well-structured content but poor analytics integrity cannot reliably detect a loss of visibility. Strong SEO practices without governed templates and accessibility controls produce fragile gains that degrade under scale. VGMM therefore evaluates whether the *combination* of governed domains produces stable external interpretation, not whether any single function performs well in isolation.

VGMM Is Unique to the Organization

VGMM scores are not assigned subjectively, nor are they generated from a fixed or universal checklist. They are derived from structured audit questions applied across each governed visibility domain, including SEO, content, performance, accessibility, automation, and measurement. Crucially, those questions are selected and weighted based on the organization being assessed. No two businesses operate under the same visibility conditions, risk profile, or discovery mechanics, so no two VGMM assessments are identical.

The questions used to assess a global public broadcaster, such as the BBC, differ materially from those used for a multinational consumer goods company, such as Procter & Gamble, or for a government entity. Business model, audience behavior, regulatory exposure, content velocity, and reliance on structured data all shape what "mature visibility governance" means in practice. For example, a consumer goods organization may place greater weight on product schema integrity, variant consistency, and structured commercial attributes. In comparison, a news or public-interest organization may place greater weight on editorial authority, authorship clarity, and content provenance.

For this reason, VGMM is inherently organization-specific. While the maturity levels are consistent, the underlying questions and their relative weights are adapted to reflect where visibility risk and opportunity genuinely sit for that organization. Domain-level results roll upward into the VGMM view, producing an executive maturity profile grounded in observable controls rather than generic best practices. Scoring is facilitated to ensure consistency, challenge unsupported assumptions, and prevent superficial self-assessment.

Because VGMM outcomes are shaped by contextualized questions and weighted judgment, publishing a single, static version of the model or its scores would provide little value and may mislead. A publicly shared VGMM, detached from organizational context, could encourage inappropriate comparison, false confidence, or incorrect conclusions about visibility readiness. The worksheets and scoring tools used in workshops[1] are, therefore, implementation artifacts of the model, not the model itself. VGMM exists to support accurate executive decision-making within a specific organizational context, not as a universal benchmark.

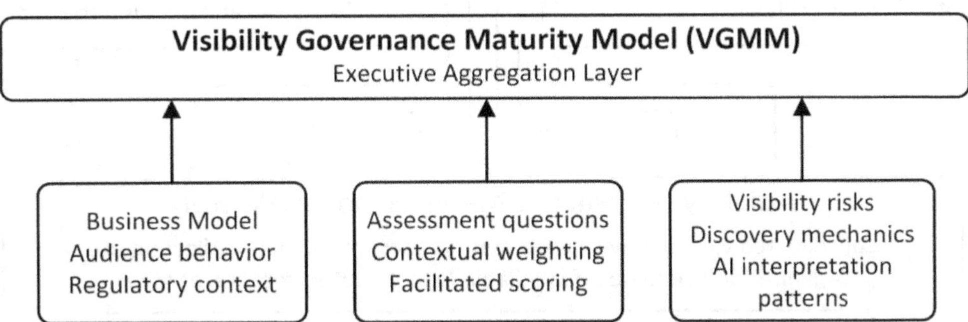

Figure 5 VGMM outcomes are derived from organization-specific audit questions and contextual weighting. While maturity levels are consistent, the assessment design reflects each organization's business model, risk exposure, and visibility mechanics.

---

[1] See https://crm911.com for the workshops

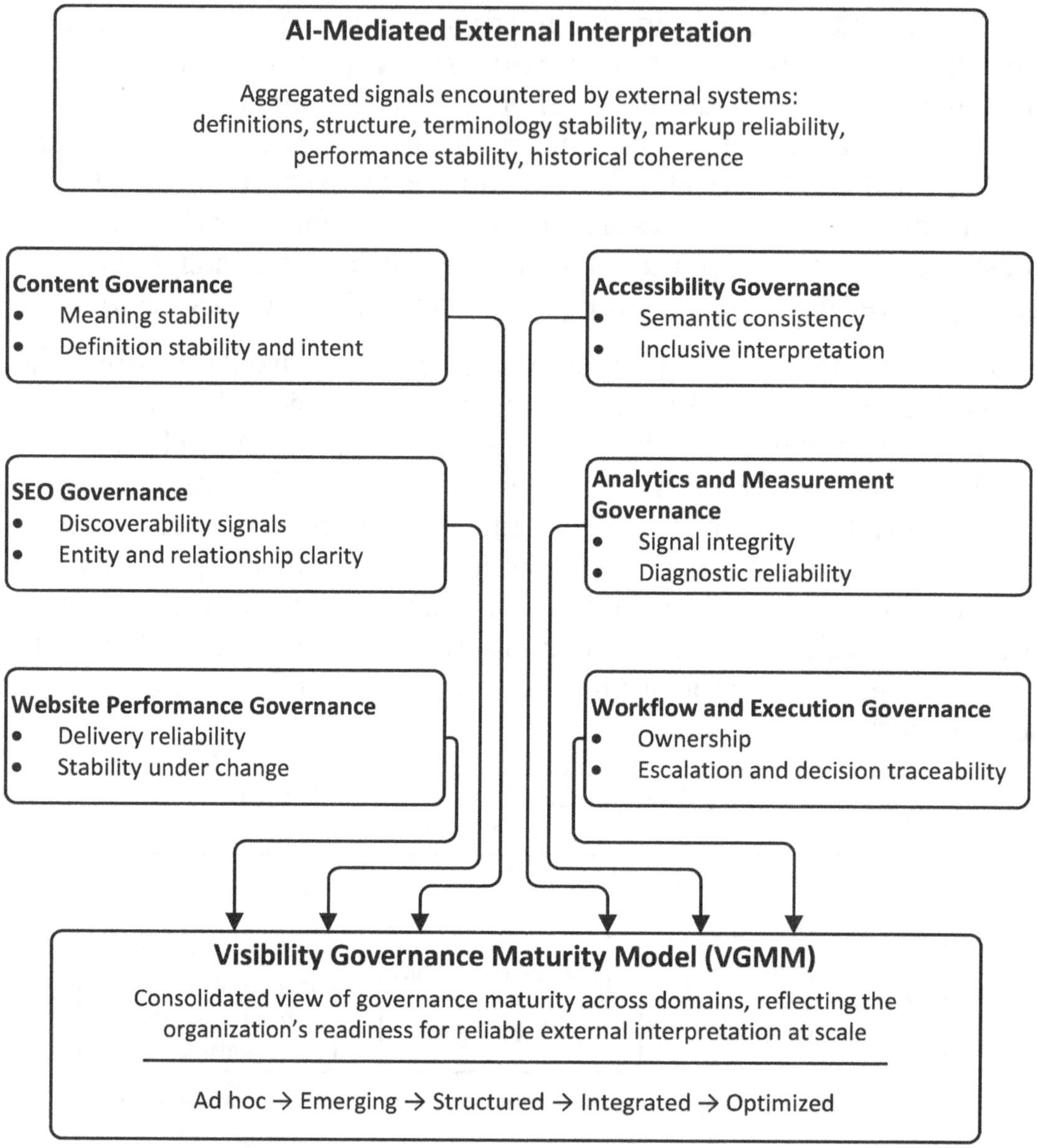

Figure 6 The Visibility Governance Maturity Model.

VGMM is designed to mirror how AI-mediated systems actually assess risk. External systems do not see internal teams or tools. They encounter aggregated signals: definitions, structure, terminology consistency, markup reliability, performance stability, and historical coherence. VGMM reflects this reality by rolling domain maturity upward into a single visibility-readiness view that exposes systemic weaknesses executives can act on, rather than fragmented operational reports.

As you read the chapters that follow, **each governance domain addressed should be interpreted as a contributor to VGMM**, evaluated through a shared maturity lens rather than as an isolated discipline. Improvements made in content governance, workflow control, technical execution, accessibility, or measurement strengthen the organization's overall visibility posture only when they are governed and sustained. VGMM provides the lens through which these efforts are evaluated collectively, allowing leadership to prioritize investment based on visibility risk rather than functional preference.

Maturity Models

Governance maturity models describe how reliably an organization can produce consistent outcomes at scale. They do not measure effort, intent, or individual capability. They measure whether disciplined behavior is embedded in the system, such that results remain stable even as people, tools, and priorities change.

The **five-level maturity structure** used throughout this book is inspired by Carnegie Mellon University's Capability Maturity Model (CMM) and its successor, CMMI (Capability Maturity Model Integration). Originally developed to assess software process reliability, the model established a widely adopted premise: organizational capability progresses through predictable stages, from improvised and reactive behavior to disciplined, integrated, and continuously improving systems.

Visibility governance adopts this same premise, while applying it to different domains. The labels used in this book differ from CMMI's original terminology, but the underlying logic is unchanged. At lower maturity levels, outcomes depend on individual expertise and local judgment. At higher levels, outcomes are produced by shared structures, enforced standards, visible ownership, and repeatable workflows.

Across VGMM and its component models, each domain is assessed against five maturity levels. These levels describe the organization's ability to maintain meaning stability, interpretability, and accountability under normal conditions and under change. An organization may be highly mature in one domain and fragile in another. VGMM exists to surface that imbalance and reveal which domains are limiting reliable external interpretation at scale.

VGMM organizes governance into domains the organization directly controls, rather than attempting to manage external platforms or algorithms. Each domain is evaluated against observable behaviors, using a **five-level maturity scale** that ranges from reactive to optimized. The focus is not on intent or tooling, but on whether consistent governance practices are actually in place.

Domain-level assessments roll upward into the VGMM view. VGMM does not replace content governance, SEO governance, website performance governance, accessibility, analytics, or related disciplines. It aggregates their maturity to provide executives with a consolidated picture of visibility readiness, exposure, and risk.

What VGMM Is Not

Visibility Governance is designed to operate at the level where strategic accountability exists, not at the level where operational detail lives. The Visibility Governance Maturity Model (VGMM) is therefore an **executive synthesis lens**, not a management or delivery tool.

VGMM does not replace domain-level governance models such as SEO Governance, Content Governance, Website Performance Governance, Accessibility Governance, or Analytics Governance. Each of those models exists to be owned, assessed, and remediated by the functional leaders responsible for day-to-day execution. Their purpose is to improve discipline within their respective domains.

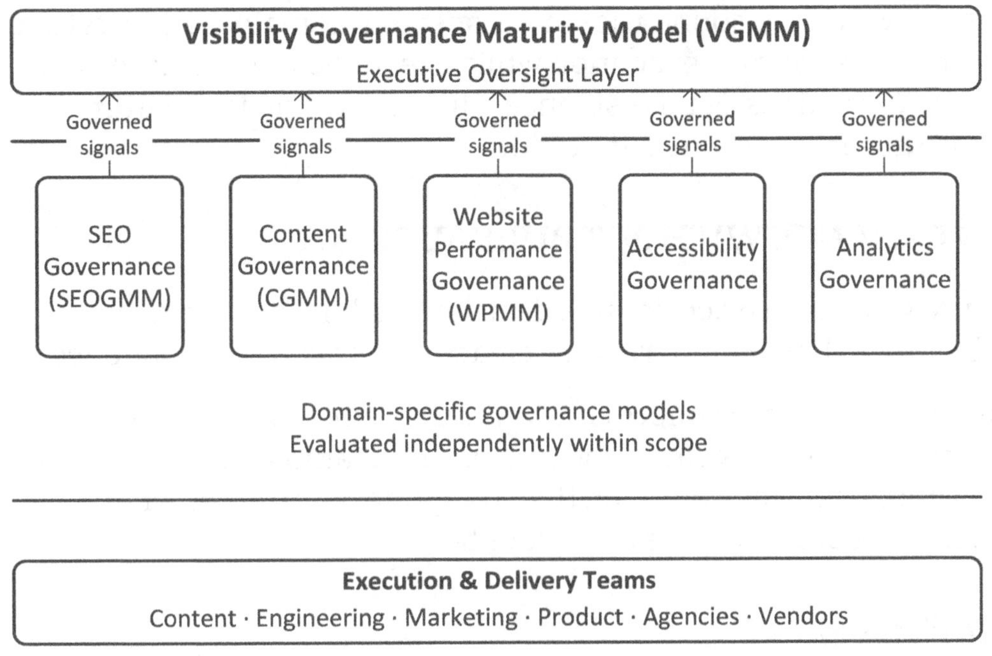

Figure 7 Visibility Governance layers

VGMM sits **above** those models and intentionally abstracts away operational detail. It answers a different question: whether the organization's combined governance maturity is sufficient to support reliable external interpretation at scale. Executives should not be reviewing domain-level maturity assessments as part of routine oversight. Doing so collapses governance layers and creates noise rather than control.

Domain models feed VGMM through governed signals—status, risk, and exception reporting—not through inherited scores or numeric roll-ups. Maturity in one domain does not compensate for immaturity in another, and no domain transfers maturity upward by default. VGMM exists precisely so that executives can govern visibility outcomes without becoming entangled in domain mechanics.

When governance boundaries are respected, domain leaders retain autonomy to improve execution while executives retain clarity over exposure, readiness, and resilience. This separation is a feature of mature governance, not a limitation.

GOVERNANCE WITHOUT BUREAUCRACY

Mature governance accelerates decision-making by removing ambiguity. When boundaries are clear, teams act with confidence.

Governance replaces improvisation with predictability. It reduces rework, surfaces risk early, and preserves meaning under pressure. In an AI-mediated environment, this discipline determines whether visibility becomes reliable or accidental.

CHAPTER FLOW

This book focuses on visibility governance as it applies to websites and AI-mediated discovery.

- Chapters 2–6 establish domain-level governance and maturity pathways

- Later chapters address monitoring, risk, and sustained operation

- Appendices provide reference material and case studies

The remainder of this chapter establishes the foundation. The next chapter moves into content governance, where visibility discipline begins at the point of creation.

Chapter 2
THE NEED FOR CONTENT GOVERNANCE

Chapter 1 introduced governance principles and cross-disciplinary structures. In this chapter, I will show you how to put those principles to work within your content teams and publishing workflows.

WHAT IS CONTENT GOVERNANCE?

If you're running a content-centric organization—a publisher, university, government department, or digital-first brand—your core value comes from the accuracy, relevance, and trustworthiness of what you publish.

In these environments, content isn't just a marketing asset. It's an operational deliverable. It shapes your reputation, your compliance standing, and your stakeholder confidence.

Content governance establishes the "3R" of rules, responsibility, and review processes that keep your content:

- Accurate
- Compliant
- Aligned with corporate objectives

It defines who decides, who approves, and who maintains content once it's published. By setting these boundaries, governance actually enables creative freedom—it just does it within an accountability framework.

A critical implication often overlooked is that content cannot be governed retroactively once it enters AI-driven systems. After publication, content may be extracted, summarized, recombined, and redistributed by search engines, large language models, and recommendation systems beyond your control. At that point, review and correction are no longer reliable safeguards.

Content governance, therefore, has to operate **upstream**—through explicit scoping of purpose, clear ownership, and traceability back to authoritative sources—before amplification occurs. Without these foundations, visibility becomes unmanaged exposure, where inaccuracies, ambiguity, or outdated assumptions travel further and faster than intended.

Good content governance doesn't constrain creativity—it empowers it. It makes sure every asset has:

- A clear purpose and audience
- A designated owner
- Documented quality standards
- Measurable performance indicators

A well-designed measurement framework lets you monitor progress against agreed goals—whether those goals are readability, accessibility, conversion, or compliance. Governance maturity grows when these measures become routine rather than something you scramble to do when there's a problem.

An additional shift that content governance must account for is the rise of **question-led discovery**. Whether through voice interfaces, AI assistants, or conversational search, users increasingly express intent as full questions rather than fragmented keywords. Content that is not structured to answer those questions clearly and directly becomes harder to interpret, easier to misrepresent, and less likely to be surfaced accurately. Governance, therefore, needs to guide not only what content says, but how it answers: ensuring that key pages resolve common questions unambiguously, state outcomes plainly, and distinguish facts from opinion. This is not about optimizing for a device or interface. It is about governing content so it performs reliably when discovery takes the form of a conversation.

CONTENT STRATEGY

An effective content strategy starts with a detailed understanding of your **audience**—what motivates them, what context they're in, and what formats they prefer. This insight determines not just what you publish, but how it's presented, maintained, and governed.

Competitor analysis adds an external lens. Studying what others publish helps you benchmark quality and spot opportunities to lead through:

- Thought leadership
- Structured information design
- Authoritative voice

In mature organizations, content strategy and governance are inseparable:

- Strategy defines why your content exists
- Governance ensures it stays reliable, ethical, and discoverable over time

CONTENT GOVERNANCE MATURITY MODEL (CGMM)

The CGMM adapts the structure of capability maturity models to digital content creation, maintenance, and oversight. It defines five progressive levels that describe how content governance evolves—from ad-hoc efforts to strategic integration.

This framework draws inspiration from the Australian Government's visibility governance guidance, with added emphasis on:

- Leadership accountability
- Cross-functional coordination
- Measurable improvement

Content Governance Maturity Levels

Level 1—Ad Hoc (Uncoordinated Approach)

Content creation is informal, often assigned to whoever's available. Editorial standards are minimal or nonexistent. The result? Fragmented, inconsistent, off-brand material that damages your credibility.

Level 2—Emerging (Not Yet Strategic)

Oversight begins to take shape. You might appoint a content manager or editor, but processes remain uneven. Silos persist, and the focus is on immediate publishing needs—not long-term quality or compliance.

Level 3—Structured (Strategically Led)

Content operations become centrally coordinated. A unified strategy and documented workflows define approval steps, accessibility standards, and brand alignment. Regular reviews ensure your published material stays accurate and appropriate for your audience.

Level 4—Integrated (Maturing Level)

Governance principles extend across departments. Responsibility gets distributed. Empowered teams apply shared content standards autonomously. Editorial, technical, and compliance functions collaborate through cross-functional committees.

Level 5—Optimized (Mature Level)

Content governance becomes a continuous-improvement system. Analytics, accessibility metrics, and structured data feedback loops guide strategic refinement. Quality assurance, automation, and AI-assisted insights sustain high performance at scale.

Few organizations reach Level 5 maturity—but progress toward it delivers real benefits:

- Reduced risk
- Faster publishing cycles
- Stronger compliance
- Improved user trust

You can use the CGMM to benchmark where you are now, set measurable goals, and plan incremental improvements across people, processes, and technology.

CONTENT GOVERNANCE COMMITTEE (CGC)

The Content Governance Committee (CGC) safeguards editorial integrity, accessibility, and legal compliance across every publishing platform. Its job is to ensure that all content—whether human-authored or AI-assisted—aligns with your organization's brand standards, ethical principles, and governance framework.

The CGC acts as a bridge between creative teams, compliance officers, and technical owners. It transforms policy into practice—making governance visible in the tools and workflows your teams already use.

Roles, Cadence, and Reporting

Your Director of Content Strategy or Chief Digital Communications Officer typically chairs the committee. Supporting members include representatives from:

- **SEO and Discoverability**—ensuring structured data and metadata consistency
- **Legal and Risk**—overseeing copyright, privacy, and disclosure compliance
- **Accessibility**—confirming inclusive design and usability
- **Brand and Communications**—maintaining message and tone coherence
- **Training Coordination**—embedding governance standards through onboarding and workshops

The CGC is responsible for:

- Defining, publishing, and updating editorial and metadata standards across all your platforms and formats
- Overseeing CGMM assessments and coordinating post-audit improvement plans
- Enforcing accessibility, localization, and inclusivity policies across departments and vendors
- Facilitating cross-functional alignment with SEO, Legal, and IT to resolve governance conflicts
- Maintaining records, dashboards, and documentation in a centralized governance repository
- Providing quarterly summaries to the Visibility Governance Committee (VGC) on risks, improvements, and training progress

The CGC meets bi-monthly during active publishing cycles and quarterly for formal maturity reviews. Major updates get reported to the VGC and the executive sponsor responsible for digital risk. All deliberations, metrics, and improvement logs are version-controlled to ensure a defensible audit trail.

Insight: A functional CGC is predictable. Every stakeholder knows their responsibility—from authors to accessibility leads. Content flows faster, governance friction declines, and your brand trust strengthens.

IMPLEMENTING CONTENT GOVERNANCE

To implement content governance effectively, start with a maturity audit. This helps you figure out where your organization currently stands and how to move toward a higher level of CGMM maturity.

Implementation does not follow a single linear path. Organizations often exhibit characteristics of multiple maturity levels simultaneously, depending on content type, team structure, and risk exposure. The goal of implementation is not to "reach" a level, but to systematically reduce unmanaged exposure by strengthening ownership, review discipline, and accountability appropriate to your context.

The maturity levels defined earlier—and detailed in the appendix— serve as a diagnostic reference. The guidance below focuses on how organizations typically begin improving governance regardless of their starting point.

Education Phase

Before changing processes, educate everyone in your content community. Everyone involved—authors, editors, developers, compliance leads—should understand:

- What content governance actually is
- Its relevance to their daily work
- How success will be measured

This phase builds shared responsibility and prepares contributors to adopt governance standards with clarity and confidence.

GOVERNANCE MONITORING CYCLE

To keep governance active—not reactive—establish a predictable review cadence. Apply this cycle across your content, SEO, accessibility, and AI touchpoints.

Phase 1—Data Collection

- Gather metrics on website performance, SEO visibility, accessibility, and AI-search inclusion
- Review compliance logs, incident tickets, and content quality scores
- Audit structured-data accuracy and policy adherence

Phase 2—Analysis

- Identify significant changes or anomalies since your last review
- Detect emerging risks: algorithm shifts, accessibility gaps, reputational trends, security issues
- Evaluate whether your prior corrective actions actually achieved their goals

Phase 3—Planning and Prioritization

- Prioritize improvements with clear acceptance criteria
- Assign accountable owners, budgets, and timelines
- Align actions with your risk appetite, legal obligations, and digital ethics policy

Phase 4—Documentation and Communication

- Produce a concise report for executives and audit committees
- Update your governance register or wiki with decisions and rationale
- Schedule follow-ups, training, or policy updates as needed

Cadence

- **Monthly check-ins:** Review algorithm/policy updates, analytics anomalies, and open risks
- **Quarterly governance reviews:** Summarize trends, recalibrate priorities, and update standards
- **Annual audit:** Validate consistent application across content, technical systems, and AI use cases

CONTENT CRISIS-RESPONSE PROTOCOL

Even with strong governance in place, content systems can fail. When that happens, you need a crisis-grade response that's fast, auditable, and aligned with executive risk thresholds.

Trigger Conditions

A content crisis is declared when one or more of these conditions are met:

- **Traffic collapse following a suspected algorithm penalty or visibility suppression**
  Example: A core update drops your top-performing content by 80 percent overnight, with no apparent cause.
- **Security or privacy breach involving published content**
  Example: A misconfigured embed leaks user data or exposes internal documents.
- **Material algorithm change that invalidates your content strategy**
  Example: Google rewrites its treatment of AI-generated summaries, and your featured snippets vanish.
- **Compliance breach with legal, accessibility, or brand standards**
  Example: A PDF flagged for WCAG noncompliance gets cited in a regulatory audit.

- **Reputational threat from published misinformation or ethical violations**
  Example: A hallucinated fact gets published as truth, or an AI-generated article gets accused of plagiarism.

Immediate Actions: Contain the Damage

Once triggered, your priority shifts from optimization to containment.

You need to:

- **Form an incident team with clear authority and escalation paths**
  Include legal, editorial, SEO, and executive comms—this is not just a content issue.
- **Establish a single source of truth for all decisions, evidence, and updates**
  Use version-controlled documents and timestamped logs. Governance lives in the audit trail.
- **Execute rollback or mitigation protocols**
  Unpublish, redirect, or revise affected assets. If needed, isolate entire content clusters.

Post-Incident Recovery: Restore Trust and Control

After containment, governance must shift to root cause analysis and systemic reinforcement:

- **Document the incident timeline and causal factors**
  Was it a workflow failure, a missed review, or an AI output that bypassed editorial checks?
- **Confirm all fixes and validate restoration of service integrity**
  Don't just patch—verify. Use structured testing and stakeholder sign-off.

- **Implement preventive controls**
  Examples: stricter editorial review of AI outputs, automated schema validation, or hallucination-detection protocols.
- **Brief stakeholders with a straightforward narrative and governance improvements**
  Frame the incident as a governance opportunity. Show what changed, what it impacts, and how you've reduced recurrence risk.

CONTENT GOVERNANCE TEAMS

Content governance isn't the responsibility of a single department. It's a cross-functional discipline that draws from both your content hierarchy and the wider organization—including Legal, Risk, and Compliance.

To be effective, your governance structure needs to coordinate across these key contributors:

- **Product Teams**
  Make sure new features and digital assets meet compliance and accessibility requirements before launch.
- **Content Teams**
  Apply approved editorial standards and metadata policies consistently across platforms.
- **Legal and Privacy**
  Verify that published material meets disclosure obligations and data-protection laws.
- **Risk and Security**
  Assess vulnerabilities introduced by automation, third-party embeds, or AI-generated outputs.

- **Executive Leadership**
  Review governance indicators and ensure resources are allocated to support maturity goals.
- **SEO Team**
  Please advise on how search engines and LLMs are evolving in their consumption and interpretation of website content.

This coordination ensures governance isn't just a policy—it's a shared operational discipline.

CONTENT GOVERNANCE COMMITTEE AUDIT EXAMPLE

To understand the current state of your content governance, your committee should conduct a structured audit using the five-level Content Governance Maturity Model (CGMM). This isn't just a diagnostic—it's a leadership tool for prioritizing improvements and tracking progress.

Here's an example of how a **completed audit** might look for an organization operating at mixed levels of maturity:

1. **Content Ownership and Roles**
   Level 2—A central content manager has been appointed, but many business units still assign writing tasks ad hoc. Ownership is improving but remains uneven.
2. **Documented Content Processes**
   Level 3—Workflows are documented for website updates, including approvals and revisions. Multimedia content isn't included yet.
3. **Strategic Content Planning**
   Level 2–3—A documented strategy exists, but its application varies. Annual planning is centralized; ad-hoc updates occur independently.

4. **Quality Assurance and Editorial Standards**
   Level 3—Editorial and accessibility guidelines are in place. Reviews occur regularly, but enforcement is inconsistent.
5. **Contributor Skills and Training**
   Level 2—Some training has been delivered, but there's no ongoing education program. Many subject-matter experts lack production experience.
6. **Workflow Integration with Other Functions**
   Level 3—SEO and Legal teams are involved in reviews, but coordination tends to happen late in the process.
7. **Analytics and Continuous Improvement**
   Level 2—Analytics are available, but few content owners use them to guide future decisions. No formal improvement cycles exist.
8. **Governance Visibility and Accountability**
   Level 2—Responsibilities are defined on paper, but reporting is sporadic. Escalation paths are unclear.
9. **Multichannel Content Governance**
   Level 2—Website content is partially governed. Social media, apps, and print operate outside formal governance structures.
10. **Cultural Adoption of Governance Principles**
    Level 2—Governance is accepted in principle, but shadow publishing and resistance persist in some areas.

Next Steps

Based on this audit, your committee can:

- Map your current state to CGMM levels
- Identify priority areas (like contributor training or analytics adoption)
- Plan targeted improvements to raise content maturity

Repeat this audit annually—or after major reorganizations—to maintain governance momentum and track your progress.

Assessing content maturity builds internal discipline. But internal process alone isn't enough. Governance must stay alert to external forces that can redefine how your content is discovered, trusted, and ranked:

- Algorithmic shifts
- Regulatory updates
- AI search behaviors

The following sections expand content governance into these wider areas of monitoring, coordination, and continuous improvement—so your governance framework stays adaptive, resilient, and strategically aligned.

ENVIRONMENTAL SCANNING IN CONTENT GOVERNANCE

Modern governance isn't just about internal control—it requires active awareness of external forces that shape how your digital assets perform and how they're regulated. Algorithm updates, accessibility standards, and AI-indexing policies can shift visibility and compliance overnight.

Good governance formalizes this monitoring so you're not caught off guard.

How Environmental Scanning Helps

- AI-driven search, social, and recommendation systems now alter your digital reach and brand exposure—often without notice
- Regulators frequently update privacy, copyright, and AI-use rules

- Algorithm transparency remains limited—so early detection helps you manage reputational and legal risk before it escalates

Governance Practices

- **Assign Ownership**
  Designate who tracks platform or algorithm changes—typically a shared responsibility across SEO, Legal, and Risk.
- **Set Review Frequency**
  Conduct monthly scans for major platforms; provide quarterly summaries to your executives.
- **Use Diverse Sources**
  Monitor official blogs (such as Google Search Central and Microsoft Bing Blogs), professional networks, and verified industry trackers.
- **Document Impacts**
  Record ranking or traffic volatility. Classify whether the root cause is algorithmic, technical, or reputational.
- **Trigger Governance Review**
  Significant external changes should prompt a mini-audit of content accuracy, structured data, privacy statements, and risk disclosures.
- **Integrate into Risk Registers**
  Each detected change should map to a governance risk item— with severity, mitigation owner, and review date.

Escalation and Reporting

When an external algorithm or AI-policy shift materially affects your visibility or compliance posture:

- Summarize the event in your next governance report

- Advise your executive sponsors of potential legal or reputational exposure
- Document your response as evidence of due diligence

Insight: Treat environmental scanning as part of enterprise risk management—not optional curiosity. Well-documented awareness demonstrates responsible oversight and helps satisfy auditors, regulators, and shareholders that your governance extends beyond internal policy.

CROSS-FUNCTIONAL COORDINATION FOR CONTENT GOVERNANCE

AI and website governance don't live in silos. They intersect multiple disciplines—and without structured cooperation, responsibility gaps emerge. Those gaps often show up as compliance failures, inconsistent content, or delayed responses to external changes.

Key Participants

- **SEO and Content Teams**
  Ensure discoverability, accurate structured data, and compliance with AI crawler policies.
- **Legal and Risk**
  Oversee copyright, privacy, and data-handling obligations.
- **IT and Security**
  Manage access, version control, and technical resilience.
- **Communications and Marketing**
  Maintain message consistency and brand alignment.
- **Compliance and Audit**
  Validate process adherence and document corrective actions.

Coordination Practices

- Schedule regular governance council meetings with all key disciplines
- Share a unified governance dashboard summarizing audits, risks, and actions
- Establish clear escalation paths when priorities conflict (like Legal vs. Marketing)
- Maintain an up-to-date contact map for rapid coordination during crises or algorithmic events

Insight: Governance fails when ownership is fragmented. Successful organizations **embed coordination into process design**—not personality—so governance outlives individual roles or projects.

As your organization scales across regions and business units, governance must evolve from informal coordination to formal architecture. Local initiatives alone can't sustain consistency, compliance, or efficiency. What emerges instead is a structured governance layer—one that defines global standards, assigns responsibility, and ensures alignment of your operations with enterprise goals.

REPORTING AND CONTINUOUS IMPROVEMENT IN CONTENT GOVERNANCE

Governance only works when outcomes are visible, and improvement is continuous. Regular reporting turns your governance work into a leadership tool—one that clarifies priorities, confirms compliance, and drives strategic alignment.

Reporting Principles

- **Clarity:** Use plain language. Avoid jargon that obscures accountability.
- **Relevance:** Focus on indicators that directly affect risk, compliance, visibility, or performance.
- **Consistency:** Use a repeatable format so trends can be tracked quarter over quarter.
- **Traceability:** Ensure every issue maps to an owner, a resolution deadline, and a follow-up.

Recommended Report Sections

- **Executive Summary:** Key insights, significant risks, and strategic recommendations
- **Governance Metrics:** Policy adoption rates, audit completion, content maturity improvements
- **Compliance Review:** Breaches, remediations, and pending issues
- **AI and Algorithm Monitoring:** Detected platform or model policy changes and their potential impact
- **Training and Awareness:** Workshops, briefings, and policy updates delivered
- **Future Focus:** Governance initiatives planned for the next cycle

DEFINING AI SYSTEMS FOR GOVERNANCE PURPOSES

Before visibility governance can be operationalized, it needs to be scoped. An "AI system," for governance purposes, refers to any software that uses machine learning, statistical modeling, or rule-based logic to generate outputs like predictions, recommendations, decisions, or content. This includes:

- Chatbots and virtual assistants
- Recommendation engines
- Fraud detection systems
- Resume screening tools
- Generative AI models (like LLMs or image generators)
- Autonomous agents and decision-support systems

Governance applies whether the system is built in-house or procured externally. What matters is the system's function—not its label. If it influences decisions, interacts with users, or processes sensitive data, it qualifies for oversight.

This definition aligns with regulatory frameworks like the EU AI Act, ISO/IEC 42001, and NIST AI RMF. It ensures your governance is proactive, consistent, and scalable across use cases.

CONNECTING CONTENT AND AI GOVERNANCE

In the VGMM, content and AI governance aren't separate—they're sequential layers of the same ecosystem.

- Content governance ensures what you publish is accurate, compliant, and aligned with your corporate goals
- AI governance ensures that the systems analyzing or generating that content behave transparently and responsibly

From the C-suite perspective, this marks a shift:

- From what your organization says
- To how your systems speak on your behalf

AI systems now mediate much of your communication—with customers, regulators, and internal teams. That makes governance not just a compliance function, but a reputational safeguard.

Next Chapter

The next chapter introduces the framework for assessing and improving website governance maturity—helping you operationalize trust in a measurable, scalable way.

Chapter 3

WEBSITE PERFORMANCE GOVERNANCE

A website that loads slowly, breaks under traffic, or fails accessibility checks is not merely experiencing a technical problem. It is exhibiting a governance failure. Performance issues are rarely isolated faults; they are symptoms of unclear ownership, weak escalation paths, and missing accountability across teams that share responsibility for digital delivery.

Your ability to deliver a stable, fast, and inclusive website experience is one of the most visible expressions of governance maturity. **Website Performance Governance** treats speed, reliability, and accessibility as shared organizational responsibilities rather than isolated engineering concerns. When performance degrades, external systems do not treat it as a localized error; they see it as a signal of operational discipline, trustworthiness, and readiness.

Website Performance Governance provides a formal structure to:

- Define ownership across technical and non-technical teams
- Set measurable thresholds that trigger action rather than debate
- Enforce accountability through continuous monitoring, escalation, and transparent reporting

To assess how consistently these controls are applied over time, this chapter uses the **Website Performance Maturity Model (WPMM)**. The WPMM is a domain-specific maturity lens that evaluates how effectively an organization governs performance, reliability, and accessibility as visibility signals. It does not replace the Visibility

Governance Maturity Model (VGMM). Instead, it operates beneath it. WPMM assessments roll upward into overall VGMM maturity, ensuring that website reliability is treated as an enterprise governance outcome rather than an isolated technical achievement.

PURPOSE AND SCOPE

The purpose of Website Performance Governance is to embed performance reliability into your enterprise's formal governance system, not as a technical objective, but as a board-visible operational commitment. Performance stops being something teams "work on" and becomes something leadership expects, reviews, and acts upon.

Under this governance approach, performance indicators become governance indicators. Site speed, uptime, and accessibility are tracked alongside financial, compliance, and risk metrics. This alignment ensures that performance failures surface through the same oversight channels as other enterprise risks, rather than remaining buried in technical dashboards.

Website Performance Governance aligns four domains of responsibility:

- **Infrastructure reliability**
  Your hosting environments, caching layers, and content delivery networks must meet documented service levels with defined escalation thresholds and decision authority.
- **User-experience speed**
  Core Web Vitals and latency objectives must be maintained across devices, networks, and geographic regions, reflecting real user conditions rather than lab assumptions.
- **Accessibility and inclusion**
  Accessibility standards and usability testing must be embedded

into every release cycle, ensuring inclusive access is enforced through process rather than goodwill.

- **Cross-functional coordination**
  IT, Marketing, SEO, Product, and Legal must operate through shared dashboards and a defined review cadence so that performance trade-offs are visible and deliberate.

By defining these as governance indicators rather than engineering key performance indicators, website reliability becomes a proxy for organizational discipline and reputational resilience.

Manager Insight
Executives often interpret performance as an engineering metric. In governance terms, it is a risk-and-reputation metric. A slow or unstable website signals weak coordination and erodes trust before any message is read. When performance metrics appear on governance dashboards, accountability expands beyond IT—and improvement follows.

GOVERNANCE FOUNDATIONS

Website performance governance begins with **explicit ownership**. Governance only works when the path from detection to decision is visible, documented, and enforced. Without named owners, issues drift between teams, and remediation becomes reactive.

Each of the following elements requires a named owner and an approved escalation chain recorded in your governance charter:

- Documented service-level targets for uptime, latency, and Core Web Vitals
- Defined incident-response roles, authority levels, and response-time expectations

- Change-approval procedures that include pre-deployment performance validation
- A scheduled reporting cadence to the Visibility Governance Committee and an executive sponsor

Visibility and responsibility are reciprocal. When performance controls appear in quarterly board or risk-committee reports, they become auditable governance functions rather than engineering afterthoughts.

KEY COMPONENTS OF THE FRAMEWORK

The operational framework translates policy into practice. It breaks website performance governance into interconnected components, each with defined owners, metrics, and review cycles. Together, these components form a closed-loop system: measure, act, review, and improve.

Performance Objectives and KPIs

Performance objectives are operational policy. They define acceptable conditions rather than aspirational goals.

Examples include:

- Uptime of at least 99.9 percent for all customer-facing websites
- Core Web Vitals rated "Good" for at least 75 percent of real-user field data
- Page-load times under 2.5 seconds on mobile connections
- Conformance with WCAG 2.2 AA accessibility standards

These thresholds provide clarity. Teams know when performance is acceptable, when it is at risk, and when escalation is mandatory.

Monitoring and Reporting Tempo

Performance monitoring must be continuous and visible. Governance defines the rhythm:

- Real-time monitoring for uptime and outages
- Daily or weekly synthetic testing of critical user journeys
- Monthly dashboards summarizing metrics, trends, and exceptions
- Quarterly governance reports covering regressions, incidents, and recovery actions

When embedded into the corporate calendar, performance oversight becomes as routine as financial reporting.

Escalation and Incident Response

Governance must define what constitutes a performance incident and how it is escalated. Typical thresholds include:

- Core Web Vitals falling below "Good" for more than seven days
- Uptime dropping below service-level targets for extended periods
- Performance degradation affecting critical conversion or access paths

Each incident triggers a documented workflow that covers ownership assignment, root-cause analysis, corrective action, and formal closure, all of which are reviewed by the committee.

Change Management

Performance governance must be embedded in enterprise change control. Any deployment affecting rendering, caching, scripts, or asset delivery requires a pre-release performance and accessibility assessment.

Approved changes include:

- A documented performance baseline
- A risk rating reviewed across SEO, IT, and Product
- Explicit rollback criteria if indicators fall below thresholds

This mirrors governance logic used in financial and compliance controls, extending oversight across the full delivery lifecycle.

Governance Dashboards

A single shared dashboard should include:

- Core Web Vitals distributions (Search Console)
- Lighthouse or PageSpeed Insights trends, including CrUX
- Server uptime and response times
- Incident frequency and resolution rates

Dashboards must be accessible beyond IT. Performance outcomes affect visibility, trust, and conversion across the organization.

Insight

Good performance governance does not chase perfect scores. It enforces consistent accountability. Metrics, owners, and escalation rules form a living system that adapts as technology and user expectations evolve.

TECHNICAL GOVERNANCE DEPENDENCIES

Website performance depends on a network of technical domains under governance. Failures rarely start in isolation. They emerge when infrastructure, deployment, analytics, or vendor dependencies operate outside shared oversight.

Integrating these dependencies under governance ensures technical decisions remain visible at the leadership level, auditable across releases, and aligned with reputational and compliance objectives.

These dependencies are rarely governed as a single system, yet failures are experienced as a single outcome. Accessibility gaps, infrastructure instability, misconfigured caching, brittle deployment pipelines, or incomplete analytics do not surface independently to users or machines. Website performance governance exists to ensure these domains are coordinated, visible, and accountable—so that performance risk is managed intentionally rather than discovered after the fact.

Access control is one such dependency. In an AI-mediated environment, performance, security, and delivery decisions do not merely affect user experience or indexing; they determine whether external systems can retrieve content at all. Changes to bot filtering, authentication, rendering behavior, caching rules, or edge delivery can prevent content from being retrieved by retrieval pipelines, even when pages remain publicly accessible. Website Performance Governance exists to ensure that such constraints are reviewed as visibility risks, with input from SEO, engineering, security, and legal stakeholders, before they suppress external interpretation. Once retrieval eligibility is lost, no amount of downstream optimization can restore inclusion.

CONTINUOUS IMPROVEMENT AND MATURITY TRACKING

Website performance governance thrives when shared discipline replaces silos. SEO owns visibility and measurement. IT owns implementation and stability. Both report through governance structures that validate alignment with business continuity and reputational risk.

Establishing Review Cadence

- Monthly reviews of uptime, Core Web Vitals, and crawl-impacting indicators
- Quarterly reassessment of performance and accessibility governance maturity
- Annual audits of infrastructure, security, and dependencies

Each review produces documented actions with named owners.

MEASURING GOVERNANCE AND PERFORMANCE MATURITY

Website Performance Maturity Model (WPMM)

The Website Performance Maturity Model evaluates how reliably performance governance is embedded across teams, workflows, and reporting structures. It measures governance discipline rather than engineering sophistication. Organizations mature by enforcing clearer ownership, escalation, and accountability—not by chasing marginal performance gains.

The WPMM uses five levels aligned with the Visibility Governance Maturity Model.

Performance Maturity Levels (Summary)

The Website Performance Maturity Model uses five levels to describe how consistently performance governance is enforced across the organization. Detailed definitions and assessment criteria are provided in Appendix A.

Level 1 — Reactive

Performance issues are addressed after impact occurs. Ownership and escalation are unclear, and responses depend on individual intervention rather than defined governance controls.

Level 2 — Defined

Performance targets and policies exist, but enforcement varies across teams and projects. Monitoring is present, yet accountability and escalation remain inconsistent.

Level 3 — Operational

Documented workflows govern monitoring, escalation, and remediation. Performance incidents are reviewed, tracked, and reported through established governance channels.

Level 4 — Integrated

Performance metrics are reviewed alongside risk and continuity indicators at the leadership level. Ownership is formalized, and performance outcomes influence planning and release decisions.

Level 5 — Optimized

Performance governance is proactive and continuously improved. Early indicators trigger intervention before external impact, and reliability is treated as assumed infrastructure rather than an operational concern.

The canonical definitions and assessment criteria for the Website Performance Maturity Model are documented in Appendix A, alongside the other domain-specific maturity models used throughout this book. WPMM scores directly contribute to the overall VGMM assessment, enabling leadership to evaluate website reliability using a unified governance language.

CROSS-FUNCTIONAL PERFORMANCE CHANGES THAT AFFECT EXTERNAL INTERPRETATION

Website performance decisions increasingly shape how search engines and AI systems interpret, access, and reuse organizational content. Many of the most consequential visibility failures do not originate in SEO execution or content quality. They originate in infrastructure and performance changes made for speed, security, or cost efficiency, without their downstream effects on crawling, rendering, analytics, or content integrity being reviewed.

Content delivery networks, web application firewalls, edge caching, geo-routing, and header manipulation operate upstream of search and analytics systems. When misconfigured, they can silently alter what external systems can fetch, how pages render without JavaScript, whether analytics remain accurate, and whether content appears consistent across regions. These changes rarely surface as immediate errors. Instead, they erode discoverability gradually, often becoming visible only after traffic loss, attribution gaps, or unexplained performance anomalies appear.

Website Performance Governance exists to prevent this class of failure. Its role is not to slow delivery or override engineering decisions, but to ensure that changes that materially affect external interpretation are reviewed through a visibility and measurement lens before they reach production.

Performance and Security Decisions as Visibility Risk

Performance optimization and security hardening are frequently treated as purely technical concerns. In practice, they are visibility decisions.

Caching rules can change the HTML that crawlers receive. Bot-filtering can block or challenge legitimate automated agents. Edge redirects and header rewriting can alter canonical signals, language targeting, or rendering behavior. Geo-routing can cause different content to be served to crawlers in different regions, fragmenting interpretation. Analytics optimizations can obscure whether content is actually being accessed.

None of these outcomes is inherently incorrect. The risk arises when they occur without visibility impact being assessed by those accountable for discoverability, measurement continuity, and content integrity. At that point, performance improvements become indistinguishable from silent visibility regressions.

SEO as a Required Consultative Stakeholder

Website Performance Governance does not assign SEO teams the responsibility for configuring infrastructure, security systems, or delivery platforms. Those decisions remain with engineering and platform owners.

What governance requires is **consultation**.

When changes may affect crawling, indexing, rendering, headers, routing, or analytics fidelity, SEO must be included as a consultative stakeholder before production release. Their role is to ensure that discoverability, AI system access, and measurement integrity are preserved—not to dictate implementation details.

This distinction matters. Visibility failures caused by unreviewed platform changes are governance failures, not execution errors. Mature organizations formalize this consultation to remove ambiguity, reduce rework, and prevent post-launch remediation under pressure.

Visibility Review as a Governance Control

In mature Website Performance Governance, certain classes of change cannot proceed without documented visibility review. These typically include, but are not limited to:

- CDN deployment or provider changes

- Activation or modification of WAF and bot-filtering rules
- Changes to HTML or asset caching behavior
- Edge-level redirects, URL rewriting, or header manipulation
- Geo-routing or regional content variation
- Performance optimizations that affect rendering or analytics execution

This review is not a technical approval gate. It is a risk-control mechanism that ensures performance gains do not come at the expense of search visibility, AI liftability, analytics accuracy, or content integrity.

Post-Change Monitoring and Shared Accountability

Governance does not end at launch. Performance changes that affect external interpretation require coordinated post-deployment monitoring. This includes crawler access patterns, false positives in security systems, analytics continuity, and unexpected regional or device-level anomalies.

At higher maturity levels, engineering and SEO share accountability for detecting and resolving these signals early. This shared responsibility reinforces the principle that visibility is shaped by system behavior, not by any single team's execution.

Performance-related visibility failures are often detected only after external systems have already adapted to them, making late correction slower, more expensive, and less reliable than early governance review.

IMPLICATIONS FOR WEBSITE PERFORMANCE MATURITY

The difference between low- and high-maturity Website Performance Governance is not tooling sophistication. It is decision discipline.

At lower maturity levels, performance and security changes ship independently, and visibility issues are discovered reactively—often after revenue impact or reputational exposure has already occurred.

At higher maturity levels, changes that affect external interpretation are surfaced early, reviewed deliberately, and monitored jointly. Visibility outcomes become predictable rather than accidental, and performance optimization strengthens discoverability instead of undermining it.

This shift is foundational to reliable AI-mediated visibility. As discovery increasingly occurs without clicks, organizations cannot rely on post-hoc analytics to reveal damage. Governance must operate upstream, where performance decisions intersect with interpretation risk.

LEARNING AND KNOWLEDGE MANAGEMENT

In the context of website performance governance, learning is not about individual skill development but about **institutional memory**: how performance decisions, trade-offs, and incidents are documented, reviewed, and prevented from recurring. Mature organizations treat performance knowledge as a governance asset, ensuring that lessons from platform changes, outages, visibility regressions, and recovery actions inform future decisions rather than being lost with personnel or projects.

Insight
Governance without performance control is theoretical. Aligning SEO oversight with IT execution converts compliance governance into a measurable driver of reliability and trust.

NEXT CHAPTER

As artificial intelligence becomes embedded in content creation, analytics, personalization, and customer interaction, governance must extend beyond performance into how automated systems shape interpretation and decision-making.

The next chapter examines how organizations govern AI use within digital operations, focusing on readiness, accountability, and the impacts on visibility rather than technical model management. It sets the foundation for understanding how AI alters discovery, trust, and zero-click decision pathways that performance governance alone cannot control.

Chapter 4

AI-MEDIATED VISIBILITY AND THE LIMITS OF GOVERNANCE

THE SHIFT FROM CONTROL TO INTERPRETATION

Artificial intelligence no longer operates only inside organizations. It now operates between organizations and their audiences. Search engines, AI assistants, and recommendation systems interpret, summarize, compare, and prioritize information before a human decision is made. In many cases, that decision is made without visiting the originating website.

This changes the role of governance. Traditional governance assumes that control is exercised over systems you operate. AI-mediated visibility breaks that assumption. Organizations do not control how external systems interpret their signals. They control only what they publish, how consistently they publish it, and whether those signals remain coherent under automated interpretation.

As AI systems evolve, **discovery is no longer limited to interpreting published pages**. Increasingly, machines discover organizations by querying structured interfaces that expose capabilities directly—such as product availability, pricing, variants, and fulfillment options—without rendering a website at all. In these environments, visibility depends less on how well a page explains an offering and more on whether systems can reliably interrogate what an organization can do. This represents a shift from document-based discovery to capability-based discovery, where interpretability is governed upstream in data and interfaces rather than downstream in content presentation.

This chapter explains why AI cannot be governed in the same way as internal systems, why visibility failures persist even after internal fixes, and why **SEO and content governance become the last reliable levers when AI mediates discovery and decision-making.**

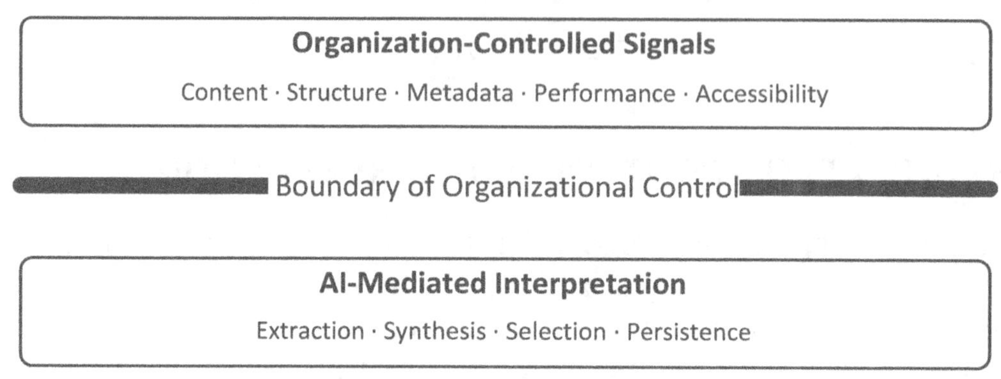

Figure 8 AI-Mediated Interpretation Boundary.

AI AS AN EXTERNAL INTERPRETIVE LAYER

AI systems involved in search and discovery do not retrieve information the way traditional engines did. They reconstruct meaning. They extract definitions, attributes, comparisons, and implied judgments from multiple sources, then synthesize them into answers, summaries, or recommendations.

From a visibility perspective, AI functions as an interpretive layer that sits outside organizational control. Once content enters this layer, it is:

- Parsed into machine-readable representations
- Weighted against other sources
- Recombined into new outputs
- Reused without reference to original intent

These systems do not understand nuance, internal context, or remediation timelines. They respond to patterns, reinforcement, and source authority. When signals conflict or drift, AI systems resolve uncertainty by excluding or deprioritizing the source that appears unstable.

Governance, therefore, cannot dictate outcomes inside AI systems. It can only determine whether the signals those systems consume are stable enough to survive interpretation.

VISIBILITY WITHOUT VISITS

AI-mediated discovery accelerates zero-click behavior. Users increasingly obtain answers, comparisons, and evaluations without visiting websites. **They may never see your content directly, yet your content influences their decisions if it is selected for synthesis.**

This breaks traditional feedback loops. Analytics capture visits, not influence. Attribution collapses while impact persists. Governance must account for this asymmetry.

From a managerial perspective, **the risk is misdiagnosis**. Declining organic traffic does not necessarily mean declining influence. Conversely, stable traffic does not guarantee continued inclusion in AI-generated answers. Visibility must be evaluated as representation, not referral.

AI systems value material that is:

- Structurally consistent
- Repeated across authoritative sources
- Easy to summarize without contradiction
- Safe to reuse without editorial risk

These characteristics are governance outcomes, not optimization tricks.

WHY SEO LOSES MECHANICAL ADVANTAGE

Traditional SEO assumed that ranking preceded influence. AI-mediated discovery reverses this logic. Selection now matters more than position. AI systems do not rank ten blue links; they select fragments of meaning.

As a result:

- Crawlability does not guarantee inclusion
- Ranking does not guarantee citation
- Optimization does not guarantee representation

SEO still matters, but its function shifts. It becomes less about competitive positioning and more about interpretability. Structured data, internal consistency, clear definitions, and stable terminology determine whether AI systems can safely reuse your material.

This is why **SEO governance becomes inseparable from visibility governance**. The goal is no longer to win rankings alone, but to ensure that what ranks is also extractable, coherent, and defensible under synthesis.

AGENTIC COMMERCE AS A VISIBILITY DISPLACEMENT

One of the clearest illustrations of this shift is agentic commerce. In this model, AI agents act on behalf of users to evaluate options, compare providers, and complete transactions without traditional browsing.

In agentic commerce:

- Discovery, evaluation, and purchase occur inside the AI interface
- Websites become data sources, not destinations
- Decisions rely on synthesized external signals rather than SERP position

This has direct implications for SEO. AI agents do not scroll. They do not compare page layouts. They do not reward keyword placement. They rely on machine-readable signals such as pricing clarity, availability consistency, reputation reinforcement, and authoritative references.

Automated replenishment, subscription renewal, and delegated purchasing further reduce user involvement. The agent's decision logic is shaped by prior interpretation rather than by real-time browsing.

In this environment, SEO rankings alone cannot protect visibility. If AI systems cannot confidently interpret your offerings, competitors with clearer signals will be selected instead—even if they rank lower in traditional search.

THE PERSISTENCE OF EXTERNAL MEMORY

A defining characteristic of AI-mediated visibility is persistence. Once an interpretation becomes dominant, it does not reset when internal remediation occurs.

Organizations often assume that fixing a problem resolves the visibility impact. In AI systems, this assumption fails. External interpretations lag internal corrections. News coverage, authoritative references, and historical signals continue to influence synthesis long after the underlying issue has been addressed.

This creates a governance gap. Internal teams may declare recovery while external systems continue to operate on outdated or dominant narratives. AI does not infer intent or improvement; it reflects evidence density.

Governance must therefore account for delayed correction. Visibility recovery requires reinforcement of authoritative signals, not just internal fixes. Silence is interpreted as confirmation, not resolution.

WHAT GOVERNANCE CAN AND CANNOT DO

Governance cannot control AI systems. It cannot instruct them to forget, forgive, or update. What governance can do is ensure that:

- Published signals are consistent across time and teams
- Ownership of meaning is explicit
- Escalation occurs before interpretation diverges
- Dependencies are visible across content, SEO, and technology

When these controls are weak, AI systems amplify ambiguity. When they are strong, AI-mediated visibility becomes more predictable.

This reframing is critical. AI is not a governed actor in this book. It is an environment. The governed surface remains your content, your structure, and your publication discipline.

PLATFORM DEPENDENCY AND THE STRATEGIC LIMIT OF GOVERNANCE

There is a final limit that governance frameworks must acknowledge: **you do not own the platforms that mediate discovery**. Even perfect governance cannot eliminate the structural risk of platform dependency.

Search engines and AI systems can change algorithms, revise policies, or shift strategic priorities without notice or negotiation. Your organization's visibility can degrade not because governance failed, but because platform incentives changed. This represents a risk category that governance can mitigate but never eliminate.

The strategic response is not to abandon search visibility—it remains too valuable for most organizations—but to treat it as one component of a diversified discovery portfolio. Organizations that combine strong search governance with systematic investment in owned audience channels (direct marketing, community building, events, subscription mechanisms) reduce their exposure to any single platform's algorithmic decisions.

This book focuses on search and AI visibility because these surfaces represent the majority of digital discovery for most organizations. However, boards and senior leaders should view the governance frameworks here as enabling—not replacing—parallel strategies to build direct audience relationships that reduce platform dependency over time.

Governance ensures that platform-mediated visibility remains predictable and cost-efficient. It cannot guarantee that platforms will continue to send traffic at historical levels. Organizations that understand this distinction invest in governance while simultaneously developing audience-ownership strategies appropriate to their industry and customer behavior.

THE VISIBILITY IMPLICATION FOR LEADERS

For executives and managers, the implication is uncomfortable but necessary. **Visibility** is no longer something you optimize after publication. It **is something you design before interpretation occurs**.

This requires abandoning the idea that governance ends at internal approval. In an AI-mediated landscape, governance extends to how meaning persists once it leaves your control.

The rest of this book focuses on the domains where organizations still have leverage: content governance, SEO governance, website performance governance, and crisis governance. These are the mechanisms that determine whether AI systems can safely reuse your signals—or whether they select someone else's.

CHAPTER SUMMARY

AI-mediated visibility shifts power away from websites and toward interpretation systems. Organizations do not govern AI itself; they govern the signals AI consumes. Once interpretation occurs, correction is slow and often incomplete.

SEO rankings, traffic, and traditional attribution lose mechanical advantage in this environment. Selection replaces position. Representation replaces referral.

Agentic commerce accelerates this shift by compressing discovery and decision-making into AI interfaces that bypass websites entirely. In that model, clarity and consistency matter more than rank.

Governance remains relevant—but only when it is visibility-first. The chapters that follow focus on the controls organizations still possess and how to use them to remain interpretable, selectable, and trusted in an AI-mediated world.

Chapter 5

SEO GOVERNANCE IN AN AI-MEDIATED ENVIRONMENT

OVERVIEW

This chapter applies the governance principles introduced in Chapter 1's Visibility Governance Maturity Model (VGMM) to SEO as a governed capability. Where VGMM establishes how governance maturity is assessed at an enterprise level, this chapter defines how SEO operates as a disciplined system of standards, controls, accountability, and review—designed to preserve discoverability, accuracy, and trust in search engines first, and in AI-mediated environments second.

SEO governance is not an extension of marketing execution. It is an operational safeguard that protects the compliance posture, brand credibility, and visibility continuity. Every SEO-relevant decision— whether technical, editorial, or automated—creates external signals that are interpreted by search engines, crawlers, and increasingly by AI systems that summarize, rank, and recommend content without direct human intervention.

Effective SEO governance ensures that these signals remain consistent, auditable, and resilient. It aligns optimization decisions with broader organizational obligations, including brand integrity, editorial responsibility, accessibility compliance, and transparency expectations. When governance is weak, SEO failures rarely present as isolated issues. They surface as a gradual loss of trust, suppressed visibility, misrepresentation in synthesized answers, or delayed recovery after change.

SEO AS A GOVERNED CAPABILITY

SEO touches many disciplines, but governance responsibility must remain explicit. Content teams may write pages, engineers may deploy templates, product teams may restructure platforms, and agencies may publish at scale. Yet, the external interpretation of those decisions converges in search results. Governance exists to ensure that this convergence is intentional rather than accidental.

A governed SEO capability establishes decision rights, review gates, escalation paths, and evidence trails. It ensures that changes affecting crawlability, indexing, rendering, structured data, internal linking, and content attribution are visible before they reach production. This is especially critical in environments where automation and AI-assisted workflows accelerate change beyond the capacity of informal review.

Governance does not slow SEO down. It prevents avoidable regression, reduces rework, and stabilizes performance over time. Organizations with mature SEO governance spend less effort recovering from mistakes and more effort compounding gains. They also reduce dependency on individual expertise. Instead of relying on a small number of experts to spot and fix problems, the organization embeds controls that prevent problems from reaching production.

WHAT SEO GOVERNANCE CONTROLS

SEO governance controls **the categories of decisions that influence how external systems understand, access, and prioritize your content.** The control objective is reliability: stable, interpretable signals that remain consistent as teams, tools, and priorities change.

Decision Rights

Decision rights define **who** can approve changes to templates, URL structures, redirect rules, structured data patterns, robots directives, canonical strategies, and metadata conventions. The practical test is simple: when a conflict occurs—engineering wants speed, marketing wants flexibility, legal wants disclaimers—who decides, and on what documented basis?

Standards and Policies

Standards convert best practices into rules that can be taught, audited, and enforced. A governed SEO standard set typically includes:

- Metadata conventions for title tags, descriptions, headings, and Open Graph fields
- Canonicalization and duplication rules for templates, faceted pages, pagination, and parameter handling
- Structured data requirements by content type and business line
- Internal linking standards that reinforce topical relationships and prevent orphaning
- Redirect and URL governance rules to preserve equity through change
- Accessibility alignment for headings, alt text, and semantic structure as interpretability signals
- Publishing workflows that define review roles and minimum quality thresholds

Workflow Gates

Workflow gates ensure standards are applied consistently. The gate is a structured checkpoint that prevents high-risk changes from moving forward without review. Mature gates are embedded in CMS workflows and deployment pipelines, so enforcement happens by default.

Measurement and Review Cadence

Governance requires rhythm. It must define when SEO risks and maturity indicators are reviewed, by whom, and what evidence is required. A quarterly cadence is common for governance committees, with monthly operational reviews for high-change environments.

AI EDITORIAL INTEGRITY IN SEO

AI-generated content introduces editorial risks that traditional SEO workflows were not designed to catch. Governance ensures these outputs do not dilute brand voice, erode trust, or create thin, misleading, or inconsistent content patterns that degrade visibility.

AI tools are now used across SEO operations, including drafting, rewriting, summarizing, generating metadata, producing FAQ answers, suggesting internal links, and creating content variants for different pages. These uses are manageable when ownership, review standards, and accountability are explicit. The failure mode appears when AI-assisted outputs enter production without control.

Your SEO Governance Committee must extend its oversight to include:

- Human-in-the-loop review: Every AI-assisted SEO asset— whether metadata, summaries, or long-form content—must be reviewed by a qualified editor before publication.
- Brand and tone alignment: AI outputs should reflect your organization's voice, values, and editorial standards. This includes terminology, formatting, and appropriateness for the audience.
- Fact-checking and source validation: Generative systems may hallucinate or misrepresent facts. External claims must be verified before use in public-facing content.
- Duplication and originality checks: AI tools often converge on similar phrasing. Duplication at scale creates thin patterns that degrade quality signals.

Governance means using AI responsibly. Editorial integrity ensures AI accelerates content creation without compromising quality, compliance, or visibility.

PRESERVING E-E-A-T IN AI-ASSISTED SEO CONTENT

Search engines increasingly adjust their content evaluation algorithms based on Experience, Expertise, Authoritativeness, and Trustworthiness—known collectively as E-E-A-T. AI-assisted content, while efficient, can weaken these signals when governance is informal.

Your SEO Governance Committee must ensure that AI-assisted outputs:

- **Demonstrate real-world experience:** Content should reflect lived knowledge or practitioner insight, especially for Your Money or Your Life (YMYL) topics such as finance, health, or legal advice.
- **Showcase subject-matter expertise:** AI can assist with structure and clarity, but authoritative claims must be backed by human expertise and verifiable sources.
- **Maintain brand authority:** Outputs should reinforce organizational credibility, using approved terminology, tone, and formatting.
- **Build user trust:** Transparency about AI involvement, clear sourcing, and editorial review all contribute to trustworthiness.

For YMYL content, governance must be stricter. AI-assisted material in these domains should not be published without human validation, source attribution, and compliance checks. This protects users and reduces reputational and regulatory exposure.

TRANSPARENCY AND ATTRIBUTION IN AI-ASSISTED SEO

AI-assisted content must be attributable for trust, defensibility, and internal auditability. Governance should establish:

- **Disclosure practices:** For public-facing content, include visible indicators when AI tools contribute. This may be a note in a footer, a content label, or a structured disclaimer where appropriate.
- **Structured data for attribution:** Use schema.org properties such as author (the human reviewer), creator (the tool), or isBasedOn (the source) where it supports provenance clarity.
- **Editorial ownership:** Even when AI assists with drafting, a named human editor remains responsible for final review and publication.
- **Internal tagging:** Maintain metadata flags for AI-assisted content within your CMS or governance repository to support auditability, performance tracking, and future reviews.

Transparency is a trust-building mechanism. Attribution ensures AI-enhanced content remains discoverable, defensible, and aligned with editorial standards.

VETTING AI TOOLS FOR SEO GOVERNANCE

AI tools used in SEO—whether for keyword ideas, content generation, or metadata automation—must be vetted with the same rigor as enterprise software. These tools influence visibility, brand perception, and compliance. Poorly governed AI can introduce bias, hallucinate facts, or misuse proprietary data.

Your SEO Governance Committee should establish a formal intake and review process for any AI-powered SEO tool. This includes:

- **Model explainability:** Understand how outputs are produced. Can the tool justify recommendations and transformations? If not, it can undermine editorial integrity.
- **Bias and fairness checks**: Ensure the tool does not reinforce stereotypes, exclude perspectives, or skew toward specific sources without justification.
- **Privacy and data usage:** Confirm that your data, including customer or proprietary information, is not used to train **external models or shared across clients without permission.**
- **Compliance alignment**: Verify compliance with GDPR, CCPA, and relevant platform policies, including search engine spam and transparency guidelines.

Procurement governance must include SEO-specific due diligence. Ask vendors to disclose risk classifications, training data sources, and mechanisms for human oversight. Document responses and review them before deployment.

SEO GOVERNANCE COMMITTEE (SEOGC)

Committee Makeup and Mandate

The SEO Governance Committee (SEOGC) provides structured oversight of search visibility, website integrity, and AI discoverability across digital properties. It ensures SEO practices reinforce visibility governance objectives, protecting brand reputation, mitigating regulatory risk, and maintaining equitable discoverability in both human- and machine-interpreted contexts.

Chaired by the Head of Digital or SEO Strategy, the committee typically includes:

- Technical SEO Lead
- Product Owner (Web Platform)

- Content Manager or Editorial Lead
- IT Engineer or DevOps Representative
- Legal Counsel or Privacy Officer
- Accessibility Specialist
- Visibility Governance Liaison (to align crawler and metadata policy)

SEOGC Responsibilities

Their responsibilities are:

- Approve and maintain enterprise SEO governance policy, including metadata, linking, and AI disclosure standards
- Coordinate with content governance on structured data depth, author attribution, and editorial standards
- Review quarterly reports on link integrity, crawl access, and Core Web Vitals
- Ensure compliance with accessibility and consent tracking requirements
- Report progress and key risks to the Visibility Governance Committee (VGC)

The SEOGC meets quarterly, synchronized with the VGC's performance and compliance dashboard cycle. Ad hoc sessions may be convened for major platform migrations, algorithm shifts, or incidents.

SEO GOVERNANCE MATURITY MODEL (SEOGMM)

The SEO Governance Maturity Model measures how effectively your organization governs SEO across people, process, technology, and accountability. It aligns SEO with enterprise goals, ensures AI readiness, and embeds compliance into daily workflows.

SEO governance does not operate in isolation. Its effectiveness is shaped by decisions made in adjacent domains—platform architecture, content systems, legal review, release management, and performance infrastructure—that SEO teams do not control but must review. When external decisions override SEO standards without consultative access or escalation rights, governance maturity collapses, regardless of how disciplined execution appears.

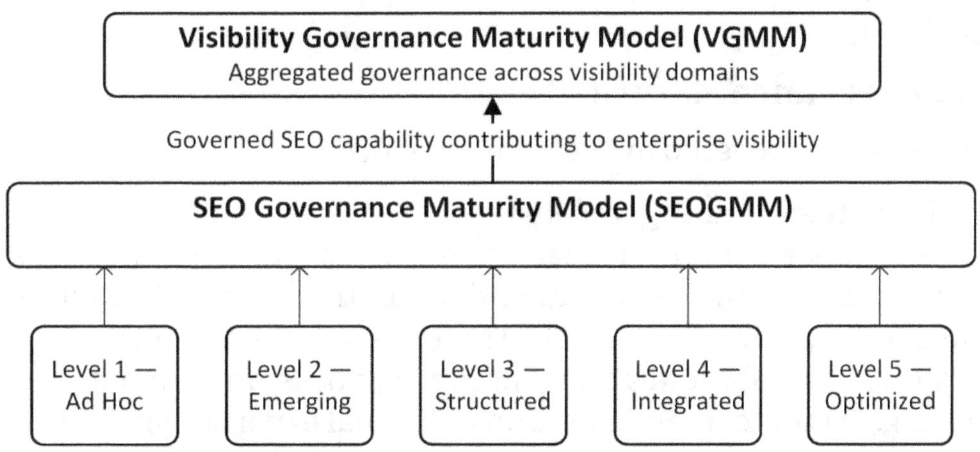

Figure 9 Relationship of SEOGMM to VGMM.

How the SEO Governance Maturity Model Works

SEOGMM is a single-domain maturity model. It evaluates how effectively an organization governs SEO as a capability, not how it performs across unrelated governance domains. Although SEO touches many disciplines—content, technology, accessibility, analytics, and website performance—SEOGMM does not inherit or aggregate scores from those domains. Instead, it evaluates how well those concerns are governed through an SEO-specific lens.

Each SEOGMM assessment is based entirely on SEO-scoped questions. These questions examine whether SEO-relevant decisions, standards, workflows, and controls exist and are consistently applied. The presence of maturity in another domain does not improve the SEO maturity score unless it is explicitly reflected in SEO governance practice.

SEOGMM produces one maturity determination, expressed across five levels. The model is inspired by the progression logic of capability maturity models such as Carnegie Mellon's Capability Maturity Model (CMM) and Capability Maturity Model Integration (CMMI), adapted specifically for SEO governance rather than software process engineering.

SEO Governance Maturity Levels

These levels are covered in detail in Appendix A.

Level 1—Ad Hoc / Unmitigated Risk

SEO governance is informal, reactive, or absent. Decisions are made in silos and validated by results rather than controls. Content quality and technical compliance vary widely. There are no documented standards, no reliable crawl and indexing controls, and limited reporting. SEO outcomes depend on individual expertise and firefighting.

Level 2—Emerging / Policy Definition

Drafted are basic standards for metadata, crawler directives, and content quality. Accountability is uneven across teams and properties. AI-assisted workflows exist but lack formal controls for provenance, attribution, and review. Some diagnostics are performed, but they are not institutionalized. Risks are recognized after incidents rather than prevented by design.

Level 3—Structured / Embedded Controls

Governance gates are built into publishing and release workflows. Templates and content types have documented standards. QA checkpoints include legal and accessibility review, where relevant. AI-assisted content is reviewed and attributable. A shared issues register exists with owners and closure dates. Performance and crawl diagnostics are reviewed on a defined cadence.

Level 4—Integrated / Cross-Functional Accountability

SEO accountability spans Engineering, Content, Product, Legal, Accessibility, and Analytics. CI/CD pipelines run validation checks for structured data, status codes, redirects, and key indexability controls. Major changes require a documented SEO review. Quarterly audits feed the VGC dashboard and enterprise risk reviews. Incident response and rollback are formalized.

Level 5—Optimized / Predictive Resilience

Governance is proactive and continuously improved. Predictive monitoring identifies risk patterns before they have an impact. Standards evolve through after-action review rather than ad hoc fixes. SEO signals are treated as enterprise visibility infrastructure. AI-mediated interpretation risk is actively mitigated through signal stability, provenance controls, and consistency enforcement. Governance remains effective through organizational change.

How to Use the Model

Use SEOGMM to:

- Assess current maturity across people, process, technology, and measurement
- Set a target maturity level for the next review period
- Prioritize high-impact improvements, such as embedding validation into release workflows and enforcing template standards
- Reassess quarterly and publish progress through governance reporting channels

Treat SEOGMM progress as risk reduction and operational reliability, not as marketing efficiency. Fund maturity gains as you would fund improvements in uptime, accessibility, and compliance.

LOCAL VISIBILITY MATURITY MODEL

For organizations with distributed retail or service locations, Local Visibility Maturity Model (LVMM) governance ensures physical presence is discoverable, accurate, and compliant.

Isolated data errors rarely cause local visibility failures. They are the result of distributed decision-making across franchises, regions, agencies, and platforms operating without shared governance. As scale increases, inconsistencies are amplified by search engines and AI systems that must algorithmically resolve conflicting signals. Local visibility maturity depends on authority, accountability, and escalation across decentralized contributors.

Local SEO Governance Maturity Levels

Level 1—Ad Hoc / Uncontrolled Liability
Location data is fragmented or unmanaged. There is no control over external citations such as Name, Address, Phone (NAP). Customer confusion increases, and liability risk rises.

Level 2—Emerging / Foundational Compliance
High-priority Google Business Profiles (GBPs) are claimed. A project begins to define a single source of truth for location data. Basic hours and review monitoring are in place.

Level 3—Structured / Master Data Control
Location data is standardized and pushed from a master system. Review workflows are auditable. Staff training is mandatory to manage reputational risk.

Level 4—Integrated / Delegated Authority

Local SEO is embedded in IT and Operations. A central system manages permissions for local teams to upload approved assets. Return on investment is tracked via booking and tagging systems.

Level 5—Optimized / Predictive Resilience

Governance is automated. Tools audit and self-correct location data deviations. GBP insights drive operational improvements and reduce reputational risk.

INTERNATIONAL VISIBILITY MATURITY MODEL

Global organizations must govern SEO across languages, cultures, and regulatory environments. International Visibility Maturity Model (IVMM) governance ensures discoverability without compromising legal or brand integrity.

In international environments, inconsistency is resolved algorithmically. Search engines and AI systems reconcile conflicting regional signals by prioritizing what appears most consistent, authoritative, and least risky to reuse. When governance fails to align definitions, structures, or intent across markets, machines select alternatives. International visibility maturity depends on consistency and governance speed, not policy awareness alone.

International SEO Governance Maturity Levels

There isn't a Level 0, but it is included below to show that some organizations forget to give International SEO its due focus.

Level 0—Unaware

No localization strategy. One website serves all markets, introducing legal, cultural, and factual liabilities.

Level 1—Ad Hoc / Uncontrolled Liability

No central policy for international domains or translation. Machine-generated content introduces brand and compliance risk.

Level 2—Emerging / Policy Drafting

Basic technical policies, such as domain structure and hreflang, are drafted. Manual translation introduces quality inconsistencies. Regional analytics are siloed.

Level 3—Structured / Global Policy Enforcement

A global governance policy defines technical architecture. Your CMS enforces standards. QA gates ensure translation quality for high-stakes content.

Level 4—Integrated / Cross-Market Alignment

Decision rights are formalized. Legal, Marketing, and Content teams define localization standards. Regional teams adapt global templates under controlled delegation.

Level 5—Optimized / Predictive and Adaptable

Governance is predictive. Automated systems monitor performance and compliance across locales. Global data informs strategic investment decisions.

HOW LVMM AND IVMM RELATE TO SEOGMM

If local or international scope applies, LVMM and IVMM function as governed sub-models that inform SEO governance maturity. They do not replace SEOGMM. Instead, they extend it by highlighting governance risks that arise only under distributed contributions and multi-market variance.

In practice, an organization can appear mature in SEO governance at headquarters while failing at the edges. LVMM and IVMM prevent false confidence by making edge-governance visible. Where the scope exists, SEOGMM should require evidence that local and international visibility controls are governed, measured, and enforced. If the scope does not exist, these models are not applied.

SEOGMM IMPLEMENTATION FRAMEWORK

This framework converts governance policy into daily SEO practice, ensuring search visibility, AI accountability, and user accessibility operate as governed controls rather than ad hoc optimizations.

Leadership and Accountability

- Appoint an SEO Governance Lead reporting to the VGC
- Define reporting lines between SEO, Marketing, IT, Legal, and Visibility Governance
- Assign ownership for key SEO domains such as technical, content, analytics, and crawl policy
- Secure an executive sponsor to ensure visibility and funding

Policy and Standards

- Maintain an internal SEO policy aligned with privacy, accessibility, and disclosure requirements
- Define how AI-assisted content will be reviewed, attributed, and labeled
- Version-control governance documents
- Align SEO policies with release management, QA, and data-retention workflows

Integration with Content and Design Workflows

- Embed SEO and accessibility review gates into publishing workflows
- Require keyword intent alignment, schema validation, and readiness checks before release

- Apply SEO, user experience, and accessibility standards concurrently rather than sequentially

Collaboration and Communication

- Hold monthly cross-team governance reviews across SEO, Content, Legal, IT, and Visibility Governance
- Maintain a shared wiki of templates, decisions, and audit findings
- Integrate SEO metrics into the enterprise governance dashboard
- Provide quarterly risk briefings to the VGC

Measurement and Audit

- Conduct recurring audits for technical SEO, content quality, accessibility, and AI visibility
- Track compliance with Core Web Vitals, schema accuracy, and crawl access indicators
- Maintain an SEO issues register with owners and closure dates
- Submit quarterly summaries to the VGC confirming follow-up actions

Training and Awareness

- Deliver onboarding and refresher training explaining SEO's governance role
- Include AI and web governance implications, such as metadata ethics and transparency
- Provide scenario-based workshops for Legal, Engineering, and Product teams

Continuous Improvement

- Conduct post-launch after-action reviews
- Update documentation and automation scripts to prevent recurrence
- Benchmark annually against VGMM to demonstrate governance maturity across domains

Insight: SEO governance succeeds when it becomes embedded in workflows rather than isolated as a checkpoint.

A PRACTICAL SEO GOVERNANCE AUDIT EXAMPLE

This example illustrates how an SEO governance audit is conducted as a governance exercise rather than a ranking exercise. The objective is to determine whether the organization can reliably preserve discoverability through change.

Audit Scope

The audit is scoped to the controls that most commonly cause visibility regression:

- Template governance for metadata, headings, canonicals, and structured data
- Crawl access and indexability controls, including robots directives, noindex usage, and canonical strategy
- Redirect and URL governance, including migration readiness and redirect integrity
- Release and change management integration, including sign-off and rollback discipline
- Content governance alignment for factual accuracy, attribution, and editorial review

- Monitoring and incident response for sudden indexation loss, crawl anomalies, and performance regression

Evidence Collection

Evidence is gathered through:

- Policy documents and template standards
- Change logs and release tickets for recent deployments
- CMS workflow configuration and role permissions
- Crawl diagnostics from staging and production environments
- Search Console and log samples for crawl access patterns
- Interviews with content, engineering, and SEO stakeholders to validate decision paths

Findings and Maturity Interpretation

Finding 1: Template changes ship without an SEO review gate. Engineering deploys template modifications weekly. SEO receives notice after deployment through performance monitoring. This maps to Level 2 behavior because accountability exists informally but is not enforced as a control.

Finding 2: Structured data is implemented inconsistently across content types.
Product pages include Organization and Product markup, but category pages and service pages vary. Validation is ad hoc, and errors persist for weeks. This maps to Level 2 to Level 3 behavior depending on whether enforcement is documented and repeatable.

Finding 3: AI-assisted content is published without consistent attribution controls.
Editors review drafts, but the review is not logged, and AI involvement is not tagged. This maps to Level 2 behavior because governance intent exists, but auditability is absent.

Finding 4: Redirect governance is strong for large migrations but weak for incremental change.
Major projects have redirect maps and testing, but everyday URL changes occur without a redirect policy. This maps to Level 3 behavior in projects and Level 2 behavior in operations, indicating uneven maturity.

Finding 5: Incident response exists but is not rehearsed.
When a visibility loss occurs, the team responds quickly, but escalation and rollback criteria are not documented, and executive reporting is improvised. This maps to Level 3 behavior for capability because integration with enterprise governance is incomplete.

Remediation Plan and Controls

The remediation plan focuses on governance controls:

- Embed an SEO review gate for template and infrastructure changes that affect indexing signals
- Add automated schema validation and status-code checks to the CI/CD pipeline
- Require AI-assisted content tagging and editorial sign-off logging in the CMS
- Standardize redirect governance for all URL changes, not only large migrations
- Define incident thresholds, escalation paths, and rollback criteria in a governance runbook
- Establish quarterly governance reporting with exception-based summaries for executives

The audit concludes with a maturity determination and a prioritized plan, then schedules reassessment to validate that controls are working in practice.

QUALITY ASSURANCE ACROSS THE GOVERNED WEB

Governance without quality assurance fails in execution. QA ensures governance policies are applied to live systems rather than remaining theoretical.

The Three Pillars of SEO Quality

Technical Integrity

Technical integrity ensures crawlers—search and AI—can access, render, and index governed content correctly. It covers crawlability foundations, indexability controls, rendering capability, and infrastructure stability.

Content Accuracy

Content accuracy ensures factual correctness, adherence to editorial standards, and validated metadata, including attribution and disclosure checks when AI is involved. It includes terminology consistency, time-sensitive claim freshness, and structured data correctness.

User Experience Quality

User experience quality confirms accessibility and performance targets are met, with Core Web Vitals and consent practices aligned to governance standards. It includes cross-device consistency and conversion pathway reliability.

Automation and Tooling

Manual QA cannot scale. Automate checks in CI/CD pipelines and scheduled audits:

- Crawl access and indexability validation
- Redirect validation and chain detection
- Structured data accuracy and regression checks

- Performance thresholds and Core Web Vitals monitoring Dashboards should feed into governance oversight, enabling transparency from technical operations to executive reporting.

AUTOMATION IN MULTI-LOCATION SEO

In enterprise SEO, automation is a governance mechanism. Managing hundreds or thousands of location pages without automation introduces risk: inconsistent metadata, broken schema, outdated hours, and off-brand messaging.

Governance-grade automation enables:

- Consistent updates across regions through structured templates and rule-based systems
- Reduced human error by minimizing manual editing of high-risk elements
- Scalable compliance by propagating policy changes without manual intervention
- Audit-ready logs through version history and approval records

Automation operationalizes governance. By embedding controls into publishing systems, you ensure that each location page meets quality, compliance, and discoverability standards.

STRUCTURED TEMPLATES FOR LOCAL SEO GOVERNANCE

In multi-location SEO, structured templates enforce consistency across local pages, ensuring standards for layout, metadata, accessibility, and schema.

Structured templates should include:

- Pre-approved layout blocks with built-in accessibility tags and responsive design
- Metadata scaffolding for title, description, canonicals, and social tags
- Schema defaults for LocalBusiness, Organization, or Service with location overrides
- Content guardrails that lock critical elements such as disclaimers and pricing formats
- Accessibility alignment for contrast, headings, and alt text, especially for location imagery

Templates reduce rework, accelerate publishing, and enforce compliance at scale. They also support automated updates, enabling changes to propagate reliably across regions.

ROLE-BASED ACCESS AND APPROVAL WORKFLOWS

Access controls and approval protocols must govern publishing workflows. Without them, unauthorized edits and inconsistent messaging can propagate across hundreds of pages.

Your framework should define:

- Role-based permissions within CMS and listings platforms. Local teams may edit hours and images, while metadata and schema remain locked to central governance.
- Approval gates for regulated content, brand messaging, and structured data changes, routed to appropriate reviewers.
- Escalation paths for high-impact changes such as pricing, disclaimers, or service descriptions.
- Publishing logs that maintain audit trails for what changed, who changed it, and when it was approved.

- Training and onboarding that aligns responsibilities to permission tiers.

Access governance provides clarity. When roles, rights, and review steps are defined, teams move faster with less risk.

DATA CLEANLINESS AND SYNCHRONIZATION IN MULTI-LOCATION SEO

Fragmented data undermines discoverability and governance. When hours, addresses, or service descriptions differ across CMS, listings, and structured data, search engines lose confidence and users lose trust.

Governance must prioritize:

- Data synchronization protocols that define how updates flow between systems
- A single source of truth for each location's core attributes
- Schema alignment so structured data matches visible content and listings values
- Change monitoring that flags inconsistencies and triggers remediation
- Governance checkpoints for high-impact changes such as closures, address updates, or service modifications

Clean, synchronized data reinforces credibility, supports trust signals, and ensures location pages perform reliably across platforms.

GUARDRAILS FOR LOCAL CONTENT AND BRAND VOICE

Local teams contribute essential context, but without guardrails, regional content can drift off-brand, misrepresent services, or introduce compliance risk. Governance ensures localization increases relevance without compromising consistency.

Your framework should define:

- Approved tone and terminology with examples for acceptable localization
- Pricing format standards, especially in regulated industries or multi-currency contexts
- Visual asset controls through approved libraries and restricted uploads
- Content boundaries for prohibited claims or regulated language requiring review
- Escalation protocols for changes to disclaimers, service descriptions, or legal statements

Guardrails reduce ambiguity, accelerate approvals, and protect the brand across every location.

QA GOVERNANCE AND ACCOUNTABILITY

QA responsibilities must be explicit. Each discipline—Engineering, Content, IT, Legal, Marketing—owns defined QA outcomes. The SEO team provides templates, training, and oversight, while execution is distributed across teams to avoid bottlenecks.

Governance is enforced through:

- Process documentation
- Regular review cadences
- Release gates and deployment checks

Measurement should track:

- Prevention rate (issues caught before production)

- Detection time (how quickly issues are found)
- Recurrence (whether the same issue reappears)
- Business impact avoided (traffic, revenue, and risk mitigation)

These metrics link QA performance directly to organizational risk posture.

GOVERNANCE RISKS WHEN ENGAGING UNVETTED SEO PROVIDERS

Hiring an outside SEO agency or consultant can accelerate progress, but it introduces compliance, technical, and reputational risks. Vendor misalignment can affect how the organization appears, or fails to appear, in search and AI-driven discovery.

Unvetted providers can violate governance policies, create legal exposure, and damage long-term visibility. Common consequences include algorithmic penalties from aggressive link schemes or thin AI-generated pages, AI visibility distortion due to poor structure and attribution, data-handling breaches from overbroad access, accessibility failures from ignoring standards, provenance gaps from undisclosed AI usage, and governance bypass through unlogged edits.

GOVERNANCE PRECAUTIONS BEFORE ENGAGEMENT

Treat SEO procurement as a governed risk process. Recommended safeguards include:

- Credential verification through case studies and method transparency
- Methodology disclosure covering automation, AI content processes, and link practices

- Visibility governance alignment across attribution, structured data standards, and access controls
- Least-privilege access with auditable edit paths
- Performance and risk reporting that includes governance indicators
- Contractual accountability defines adherence, disclosure, remediation responsibility, and confidentiality

Insight: In an AI-driven discovery environment, the wrong SEO partner can harm not only rankings but also representation inside synthesized answers.

SEO CONTRACT GOVERNANCE

When external partners contribute, their work must operate within the same governance boundaries as internal teams. Contract governance ensures outside contributors reinforce standards for accuracy, accessibility, attribution, structured data, and content integrity.

Governed SEO contracts focus on alignment. They require transparency in methods, disclosure of automation, clarity in data handling, and commitment to internal review workflows. They specify evidence expectations such as validation results, change logs, and acceptance notes, rather than prescribing every technical detail.

Contracts reduce risk by clearly stating prohibited practices. Link schemes, undisclosed AI-generated content, scraping, and attempts to bypass QA controls are not acceptable. Access governance should specify least-privilege permissions, traceability of edits, and removal of access at project completion. Contract governance links vendor activities to SEOGC reporting rhythms so outcomes and risks remain visible.

EXECUTIVE QA SIGN-OFF AS A GOVERNANCE CONTROL

Major releases require a governance-grade sign-off process. This is not an executive review of technical detail. It confirms that the controls that protect visibility have been applied and validated.

Before major releases, confirm:

- Access and indexing: key pages are discoverable and indexable
- URLs and redirects: mapped, tested, and monitored
- Templates and metadata: render correctly and structured data validates
- Experience: conversion paths meet performance and accessibility targets
- Monitoring and rollback: alerts configured, owners named, rollback documented

Executive sign-off creates accountability for protecting visibility during change, ensuring that operational velocity does not override governance discipline.

Chapter 6
LINK GOVERNANCE

OVERVIEW

Link governance ensures that every inbound and outbound link across your digital ecosystem is ethical, accessible, and compliant with both search-engine standards and legal obligations.

Oversight belongs to the SEOGC, which makes sure linking strategies align with:

- Ethical marketing practices
- Corporate policy
- Enterprise governance objectives

While operational link management remains decentralized—across SEO, content, and technical teams—all policy decisions, exceptions, and link-related risks must remain visible to the committee for coordinated oversight.

LINK GOVERNANCE FOUNDATIONS

Effective link governance begins with purpose and responsibility. Its core objectives are to:

- Protect your brand reputation
- Prevent link-based SEO penalties
- Support authenticity across all your digital properties

The SEOGC should:

- Approve the initial Link Governance Playbook
- Endorse ownership assignments
- Review updates annually as part of its governance reporting cycle

To establish a foundation:

- Define link governance objectives: Reputation protection, accessibility assurance, SEO compliance.
- Ensure linked content meets WCAG standards or carries appropriate warnings.
- Assign ownership across SEO, Legal, Content, and IT, with escalation paths for broken or questionable links.
- Document approval workflows for sponsored, affiliate, or partnership links.
- Maintain a governance playbook outlining audit frequency, approval processes, and recordkeeping practices.

INBOUND LINK OVERSIGHT

Inbound links are public trust signals. Governance ensures they're earned ethically and don't expose your organization to penalties or reputational risk.

Key Responsibilities

Monitor link quality and referring-domain reputation using tools like Majestic, Ahrefs, SEMrush, or Google Search Console.

Flag links from low-authority, spam-heavy, or irrelevant domains.

Define thresholds for disavowal—based on domain authority, anchor-text patterns, or unnatural link velocity.

Document each disavow decision with a rationale and maintain a governance log.

Review link-building campaigns quarterly for compliance with Google's guidelines and ethical standards.

Identify and mitigate link networks, reciprocal schemes, or paid exchanges.

OUTBOUND LINK GOVERNANCE

Every outbound link is an editorial endorsement. Governance ensures these signals remain trustworthy, accessible, and policy-aligned.

Governance Priorities

Maintain an outbound-link policy distinguishing editorial, partner, and sponsored links.

Require rel="nofollow" or rel="sponsored" attributes for paid or affiliate relationships.

Ensure outbound links serve clear informational or reference purposes.

Conduct accessibility and compliance checks for linked content.

Avoid inaccessible PDFs or non-compliant forms.

Automate scans for broken or redirected links and route repair tasks to content owners.

Periodically review outbound links for relevance and remove any obsolete or off-brand references.

TECHNICAL AND STRUCTURAL CONTROLS

Link governance depends on strong technical controls within your CMS and analytics systems.

Core Practices

Validate structured data and schema markup where outbound links appear (like sameAs, author).

Standardize UTM parameters and campaign tags to prevent analytics noise.

Maintain documentation standards for tracking codes and naming conventions

Lock down link fields in CMS templates to prevent unauthorized edits.

Use automated scripts or macros to validate link formatting, status codes, and attribute consistency during QA.

DOCUMENTATION AND TRAINING

Governance endures only when knowledge is shared and reinforced.

Recommended Actions

Maintain a Link Governance Playbook with audit checklists, approval workflows, and escalation steps.

Map link types to risk levels, defining who approves what and when

Train content and marketing teams on anchor-text best practices, disclosure requirements, and link hygiene.

Include examples of compliant vs. risky linking behavior to build confidence and awareness.

COMMITTEE OVERSIGHT

The SEO Governance Committee should review quarterly link-governance reports summarizing:

- Inbound quality metrics
- Outbound compliance checks
- Disavow actions

It must verify that link practices across business units remain consistent with corporate policy—and that vendors adhere to declared ethical standards.

MEASUREMENT AND ACCOUNTABILITY

Metrics should emphasize integrity, not volume.

Suggested Indicators

Percentage of backlinks from authoritative, relevant domains

Number of disavowed or toxic links identified per quarter

Ratio of earned vs. solicited backlinks

Frequency of outbound link audits and average remediation time

Compliance rate with sponsored-link disclosure policies

Insight: Link governance is both a reputational shield and an operational discipline. When overseen appropriately, it transforms link management from an SEO tactic into an expression of organizational integrity.

Chapter 7

MEASUREMENT AND REPORTING

When AI systems evaluate organizations through direct data queries rather than page visits, traditional visibility indicators lose explanatory power. Discovery, comparison, and even transaction selection may occur without generating a session, impression, or referral. In such cases, the absence of traffic does not indicate the absence of influence—it indicates that interaction has moved beyond observable surfaces. Measurement frameworks that remain page-centric, therefore understate both opportunity and risk, reinforcing the need for governance models that account for visibility without visits.

THE MEASUREMENT HIERARCHY

Strong measurement is the feedback loop of governance. In digital and AI-enabled organizations, it confirms whether your website, content, and AI-system policies are producing their intended outcomes.

Not every metric deserves equal weight. Organize them hierarchically:

Level 1—Business Outcomes
These are the metrics your board and executives care about most: revenue from organic search, customers acquired through organic channels, share of voice in search visibility, and cost-per-acquisition from organic activity.

Level 2—Performance Indicators
These correlate strongly with outcomes but are one step removed: qualified organic traffic, conversion rate, rankings for high-value keywords, and engagement metrics like average engagement time per session.

Level 3—Health Metrics

These measure the conditions that enable sustained performance: indexation rate, crawl efficiency, page speed, and Core Web Vitals.

Level 4—Activity Metrics

These track operational effort: content published, technical issues resolved, links acquired, and pages optimized.

NORTH STAR METRICS—YOUR GUIDING LIGHT

Your North Star Metric (NSM) is the single measure that best reflects the value SEO delivers to your organization. It anchors visibility, accessibility, and compliance alongside commercial outcomes.

A good NSM is directly correlated with business value, influenced by SEO actions, measured consistently, easily understood by non-SEO stakeholders, and acts as a leading indicator—not a lagging one.

Examples by Business Model

- **E-commerce:** Revenue from organic search

- **Lead generation:** Qualified leads from organic search

- **Subscription services:** Free-to-paid conversions from organic traffic

- **Publishers:** Engaged minutes from organic search

- **B2B:** Pipeline value influenced by organic search

Common Pitfalls

Don't fall into these traps: choosing organic traffic (which is an input, not an outcome), selecting metrics that SEO cannot directly affect (like total company revenue), or picking overly narrow metrics that fail to guide strategy.

The best NSM moves are often enough to steer your actions without becoming noise.

TRAFFIC METRICS BY INTENT AND QUALITY

Organic traffic remains essential, but it must be interpreted through the lens of digital responsibility. Governance standards increasingly require indicators for accessibility, consent, and content accuracy.

You should segment traffic by branded vs. non-branded searches, device type, user intent, key page types, and new vs. returning visitors. A 10 percent overall increase may mask a 30 percent decline in high-value commercial traffic.

Branded vs. Non-Branded Traffic

Branded traffic comes from searches for your company or product names. Non-branded traffic comes from discovery queries.

Typical branded traffic ratios look like this: established brands see 60–80 percent, growing brands see 40–60 percent, and newcomers see 10–30 percent. Use Google Search Console and GA4 landing page data to approximate your branded splits.

Traffic by Search Intent

Different search intents serve different funnel stages. Informational queries build awareness, navigational queries show destination intent, commercial investigation queries indicate comparison behavior, and transactional queries signal purchase intent. Balanced intent coverage nurtures your whole funnel.

Quality Over Quantity

Prioritize these indicators: engagement rate, bounce rate, pages per session, average engagement time, conversion rate, and repeat-visitor frequency. Relevance beats reach every time—tie traffic quality back to revenue and lead quality.

RANKING AND CONVERSION METRICS

Keyword rankings provide direction, not outcomes. Track representative keywords segmented by intent, benchmarked against competitors, and use entity-level tracking if available.

Conversions matter most. Macro conversions include purchases, form submissions, and trial sign-ups. Micro conversions include downloads, newsletter sign-ups, and video views.

Use multiple attribution models—last-click, first-click, linear, position-based, data-driven—for richer insight.

These metrics should flow upward into your Website Governance Committee reviews—confirming that SEO supports strategic and ethical principles across AI and content governance.

AI-ERA METRICS

AI search introduces new challenges. Visibility often occurs without a click.

You need to track brand-mention frequency across AI assistants (ChatGPT, Gemini, Perplexity, Copilot), citation format (URL vs. reference), and sentiment and share of AI visibility vs. competitors.

Use proxy metrics, such as branded search volume trends, spikes in direct traffic, and customer surveys, to identify AI assistants as discovery channels.

Your Visibility Governance Committee should review these reports to ensure brand representation aligns with policy and ethical standards.

As AI-mediated discovery becomes increasingly context-aware, attempts to track universal "AI rankings" or fixed synthesis outputs become misleading. **Large language models do not produce a single canonical answer that all users see.** They adapt responses based on industry context, prior interactions, role assumptions, and inferred intent. The result is that two executives asking the same question may receive materially different answers, each optimized for their perceived needs. In such an environment, position tracking shifts from being incomplete to being structurally invalid. Governance focus must therefore move away from observing isolated outputs and toward ensuring that the organization's content, expertise, and authority remain consistently trustworthy across contexts that cannot be directly inspected.

For executives, this means that governance maturity is revealed not by what a single AI interface displays today, but by whether the organization is **consistently selected** when interpretation varies tomorrow.

AI SEO METRICS AND CONTENT ACCOUNTABILITY

As AI-assisted content becomes common, measurement must evolve beyond ranking and traffic. The goal is not only to know whether your pages attract clicks, but also whether they demonstrate integrity, usefulness, and trust once visitors arrive.

Traditional performance dashboards show how much attention you earned. AI SEO metrics reveal whether that attention was deserved. These signals help you govern the quality and responsibility of your AI-driven content systems.

Measuring Utility and Integrity

AI can accelerate production, but it can also dilute quality if governance guardrails are weak. Use post-click and authority-based indicators to confirm that AI supports—not undermines—your brand credibility.

1. Utility and Helpfulness—Time to Answer

Measure how quickly a visitor finds the key information they came for. A slow "time to answer" usually indicates that AI-generated text is wordy or that its structure hides the main point. Governance reviews can flag these pages for revision.

2. Trust and Brand Recall—Branded to Non-Branded Search Ratio

Track the share of searches that include your brand name. A rising branded-search ratio signals that people remember your content as reliable. It's a practical proxy for authority and trust.

3. Engagement and Authenticity—Dwell Time and Pogo-Sticking

Monitor how long users stay before returning to search results. Short visits or high pogo-sticking suggest the page failed to satisfy intent. When AI content repeats surface information, users leave quickly. These metrics help you identify pages that need stronger insight or originality.

4. Visibility Versus Value—Click-Through Rate from AIO or Featured Snippets

In AI-enhanced results, visibility alone isn't enough. Track how often users click from Google's AI Overviews (AIO) or other summary panels to your site. A low rate indicates your title or description lacks a clear differentiating benefit.

5. Authority and Expertise—E-E-A-T Consistency Audits

Audit AI-assisted pages for authorship, citations, and evidence. Transparent sourcing and expert attribution remain essential governance safeguards for factual accuracy and brand credibility.

Treat these as trust indicators rather than vanity metrics. They reveal whether your AI content process is working as intended.

Monitoring AI Impact on Rankings and Indexation

AI-generated content can influence search performance in unpredictable ways. Governance prevents ranking volatility, crawl inefficiencies, or even deindexation—especially if content lacks originality, structure, or editorial oversight.

Your SEO Governance Committee should establish monitoring protocols for AI-assisted content. Start by internally flagging AI-generated pages or sections in your CMS—this lets you isolate performance trends and audit content lineage. Monitor ranking fluctuations for AI-assisted pages, since sudden drops may indicate quality issues, duplication, or algorithmic penalties. Use log files and crawl stats to detect changes in crawl frequency, depth, or prioritization. And regularly audit which AI-assisted pages are indexed, excluded, or flagged.

Establishing Oversight Thresholds

Your governance committees can set minimum acceptable thresholds for each metric—such as average dwell time, branded-search share, or AI Overview click-through rate.

Pages that fall below these thresholds should trigger manual review to verify structure, originality, and factual clarity. Link these reviews to your regular Visibility Governance Committee meetings so actions are documented and traceable. AI SEO metrics work as an early warning system—they show you whether automation is enhancing or eroding your content quality.

Checklist—AI SEO Governance Readiness

Use this checklist to confirm that your organization measures AI-era performance responsibly:

- Do your dashboards track both visibility (citations, mentions) and utility (time to answer, dwell time)?
- Are AI-generated or AI-assisted pages reviewed for E-E-A-T compliance before publication?
- Have you defined a minimum engagement benchmark to detect weak or generic AI copy?
- Is branded-search growth included in quarterly governance reviews as a trust indicator?
- Are underperforming AI pages assigned clear corrective actions and ownership?

These checks elevate AI SEO from a tactical exercise to a management discipline, ensuring automation operates within clear, measurable, and ethical boundaries.

COMPETITIVE BENCHMARKING

Benchmarking provides context. Compare your share of voice, content velocity, technical health, link profile, and AI visibility against competitors.

Benchmark results should inform both your website-performance and AI-governance scorecards—reinforcing that competitive advantage and compliance maturity advance together.

REPORTING AND VISUALIZATION

Data without insight is decoration. Reporting turns measurement into action.

Your monthly dashboards should align with governance cycles.

Effective Reports Include

A good report starts with an executive summary covering performance vs. goals, key developments, and planned responses. Include your NSM trend, segmented KPIs for traffic, rankings, and conversions, competitive context, next-month priorities, and explicit decisions needed from stakeholders.

Example Visualization

An executive dashboard should connect your NSM with supporting KPIs and trend lines, use line charts for trends and bar charts for comparisons, apply restrained color for emphasis, and prioritize clarity over decoration.

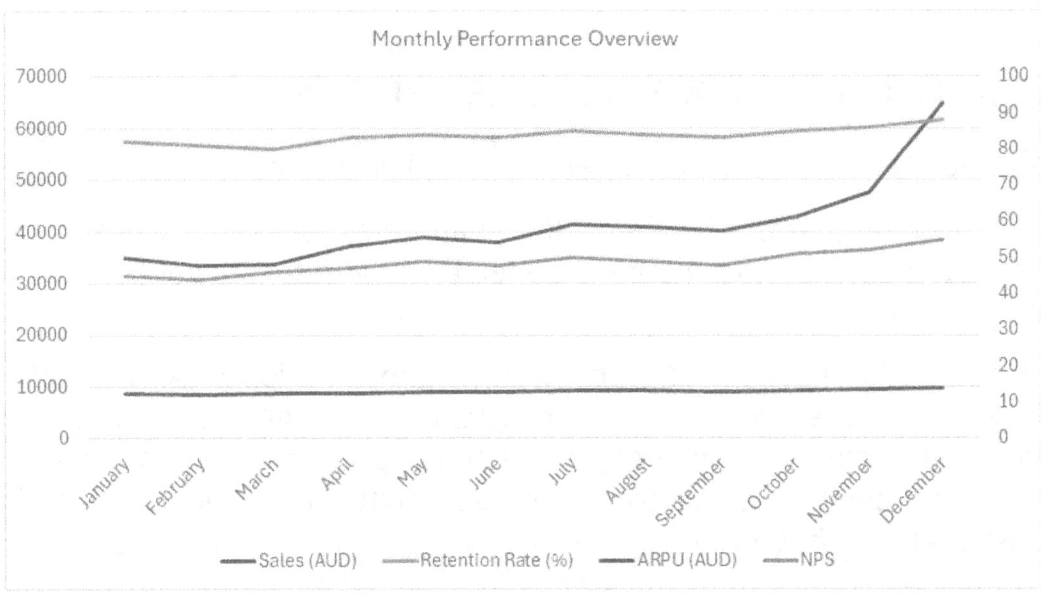

Figure 10 Executive dashboard highlighting NSM, 3 KPIs, and trend lines.

Avoid vanity metrics, data dumps, and buried performance issues. Clarity drives responsibility.

FRAMEWORK FOR MEASUREMENT MATURITY

A mature measurement program balances metric selection, data quality, analysis capability, reporting effectiveness, and AI-era readiness.

This assessment should inform your Visibility Governance Council's annual review, ensuring measurement evolves under oversight.

Evolving Your Measurement Framework

Measurement must evolve with technology and behavior. Treat it as a living system.

Quarterly reviews should ask: Are we still measuring the right things? Annual reviews should audit your tools, NSM validity, and peer benchmarks.

WHEN METRICS DON'T TELL THE WHOLE STORY

Dashboards explain what happened—not always why.

Balance your quantitative data with qualitative inputs such as user surveys, customer interviews, sales feedback, support ticket trends, and session recordings.

SEO also influences brand perception, market positioning, competitive defense, and even talent attraction. Qualitative insight helps your governance committees interpret the human outcomes behind the numbers—connecting measurement back to the actual decisions and trust-building that matter.

THE MEASUREMENT MINDSET

Effective measurement demands both skepticism and humility. Mature governance cultures treat analytical rigor as a safeguard—

validating not just outcomes, but the integrity of the systems that produced them.

Question anomalies. Distinguish correlation from causation. Accept uncertainty. Focus on trends, not isolated data points. Use findings to learn—not to justify. Share metrics openly to enable collective insight.

CONNECTING MEASUREMENT TO ACTION

Metrics without action are academic.

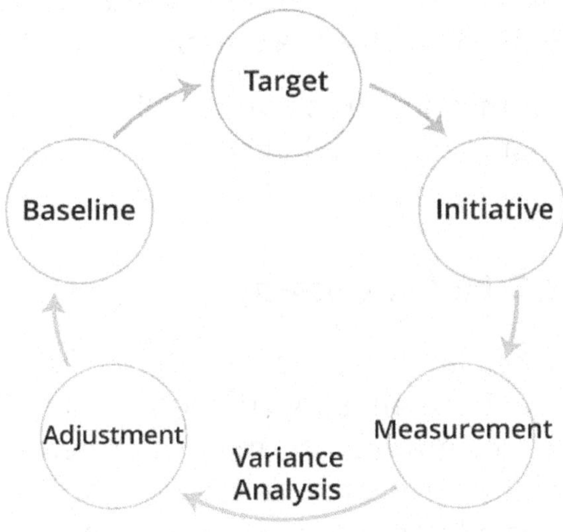

Figure 11 Governance loop.

Every metric should have a defined response. When performance exceeds expectations, document success drivers and scale. When it meets expectations, maintain and monitor. When it misses expectations, trigger corrective action.

Embedding this loop into governance reporting ensures corrective actions are documented, owned, and reviewed across AI and website domains.

MEASUREMENT IN CRISIS SITUATIONS

When performance drops suddenly, measurement becomes diagnostic.

Here are the steps to take: verify the drop, determine its scope, identify potential causes (like algorithm updates or deployment errors), conduct segmentation and technical audits, document timelines, and develop testable hypotheses.

Crisis reporting should trigger immediate escalation to the relevant governance committee—typically your Website Performance Committee or Visibility Governance Committee.

Transparent communication preserves credibility. Tell stakeholders what happened, what is known, what is unknown, and what is being done.

The Future of SEO Measurement

The SEO measurement landscape is evolving rapidly. AI assistants mediate more interactions, making attribution complex. Privacy regulations reduce data granularity, making directional trends more important. Multi-platform and predictive analytics replace static reports. Real-time dashboards shorten feedback loops—but require interpretive restraint.

In the era of Visibility Governance, SEO measurement operates as a marketing function, a compliance validator, a reputational safeguard, and a transparency checkpoint all at once.

Chapter 8

GOVERNANCE WORKFLOWS FOR AI VISIBILITY

You manage visibility by shaping how work moves through your organization. Governance workflows translate visibility goals into predictable actions across content, product, design, and engineering, enabling teams to release changes that search engines and artificial intelligence systems can consistently interpret. The value of governance workflows is not bureaucracy. The value is stability: the same intent expressed in the same way, release after release, page after page, and team after team. When workflows are explicit, drift is reduced, avoidable rework is prevented, and the time between detecting a visibility risk and correcting it shortens materially.

This chapter focuses on operational clarity. It describes the standard workflow pattern that underpins AI-visible delivery, explains how decision rights and escalation operate inside that pattern, and shows how quality expectations can be embedded into everyday tools. The aim is not to introduce new processes, but to make existing ones legible, repeatable, and resilient under change.

WORKFLOW PURPOSE

Governance workflows anchor visibility in structure rather than improvisation. They establish a shared understanding of what must be checked, who must be consulted, and what "done" means before work moves forward. This matters because machines interpret patterns rather than intent. A human reader can tolerate small inconsistencies in labels, summaries, or page structure. Machine interpretation is far less forgiving. When the same concept is expressed inconsistently across pages or releases, systems that summarize, compare, and recommend may fragment that meaning or misclassify it entirely.

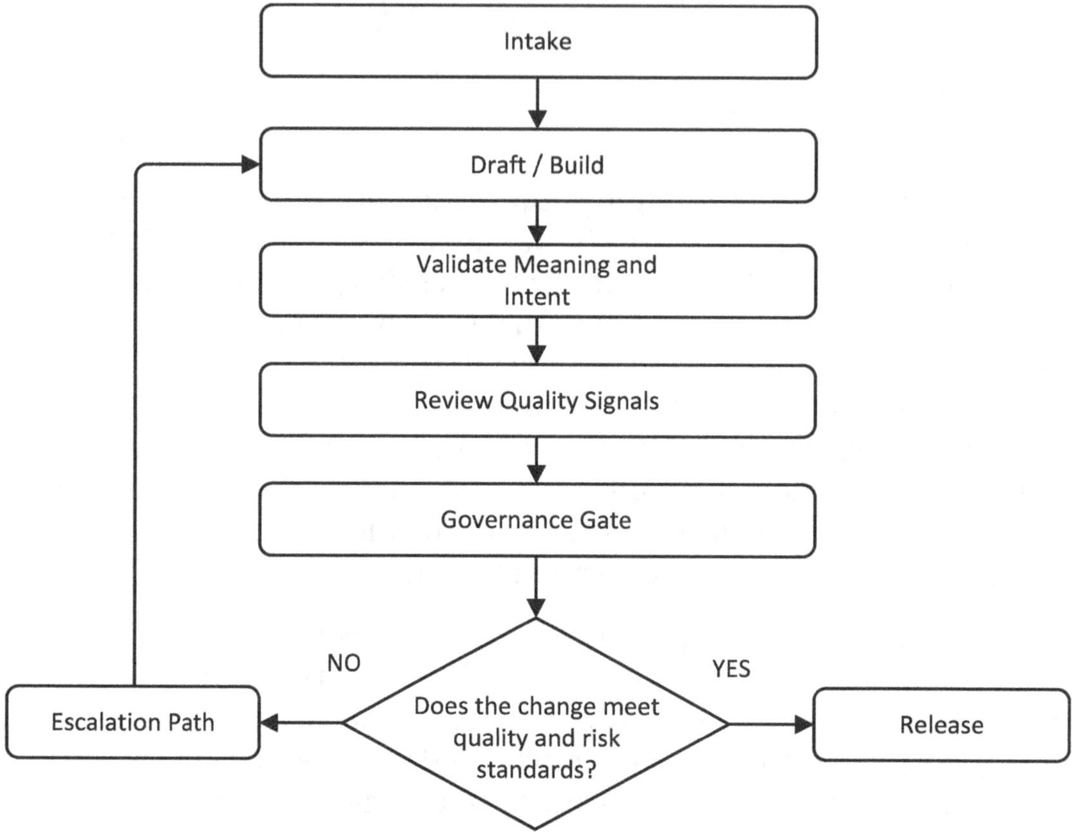

Figure 12 Core Governance Workflow for AI Visibility

Figure 12 shows the core governance workflow for AI visibility. It represents the standard path a change follows from initial definition through release and post-release learning. The purpose of this workflow is not to slow delivery, but to stabilize meaning while work moves quickly. Contributors should be able to ship with confidence because expectations are visible, standards are accessible, and accountability is clear. When the path is known, governance stops feeling like an external requirement and becomes an uncertainty-reduction mechanism.

Workflows also protect against the most common source of visibility failure: informal pathways. Small technical changes made outside release processes, content updates published before metadata validation, or template drift caused by disconnected design and engineering decisions are not edge cases. They are predictable outcomes of missing coordination. A governance workflow exists to make coordination the default behavior rather than the exception.

WORKFLOW FOUNDATIONS

Governed workflows remain effective only when they reflect how work actually happens. A theoretically correct workflow that conflicts with the delivery rhythm will be bypassed under pressure. A lightweight workflow that is clearly owned and integrated into existing practices will be used because it makes work easier. The foundation of a workflow is therefore a design problem rather than a documentation exercise. It defines how decisions and checks travel through the organization.

A stable workflow foundation includes a recognizable sequence that contributors can follow without explanation. That sequence typically begins with defining the scope and expected impact of a change, continues through creation or implementation against shared standards, incorporates validation of intent, accessibility, metadata, and structured meaning, and applies review and approval thresholds that reflect risk. The workflow concludes with monitored release and learning that feeds back into standards and decision records. Making this sequence explicit does not add work. It exposes omissions early, when they are cheapest to correct.

Foundations must also account for intent. AI-mediated visibility depends heavily on whether content aligns with real user tasks and language. A workflow that validates structure while ignoring intent will consistently produce pages that are technically correct but semantically weak. Intent validation is therefore a workflow requirement, not a stylistic preference, because it determines whether content resolves queries clearly when interpreted by machines.

DECISION PATHS AND ACCOUNTABILITY BOUNDARIES

Clear decision paths eliminate the guesswork that causes delay and rework. Each decision requires a single accountable owner, even when several teams participate in review. Accountability is not about authority. It is about coordination. When contributors know who owns a decision, escalation happens earlier, conflicts resolve faster, and reversals after release become less common.

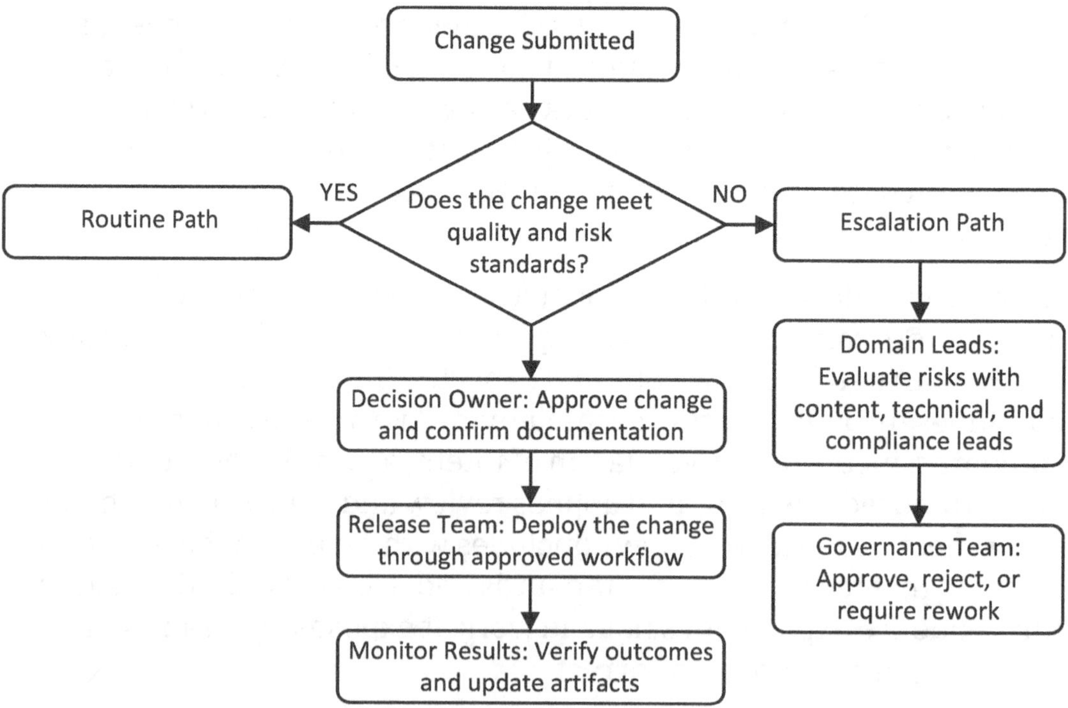

Figure 13 Decision and Escalation Paths

Figure 13 illustrates decision and escalation paths within a governed workflow. In practice, decision rights are distributed across domains. Content owners are accountable for narrative clarity and factual integrity. Product owners define the page's purpose and align it with user tasks. Design owners shape usability and scanning behavior. Engineering owners ensure technical feasibility and quality. SEO owners safeguard meaning alignment and discoverability signals. These domains overlap intentionally. The workflow must specify how conflicts are resolved when priorities collide, since conflicts are common in complex environments.

Explicit decision paths also support auditability. When ownership is clear, it becomes possible to trace why a change was made, who approved it, and which standard it relied on. This traceability is essential when diagnosing regressions, explaining shifts in AI-generated summaries, or understanding why a page cluster drifted from its intended structure.

QUALITY SIGNALS THAT PROTECT EXTERNAL INTERPRETATION

Quality signals translate abstract expectations into concrete, repeatable checks that protect meaning as work moves through the workflow. Machines consistently reward clarity, consistency, structure, and reliability because those attributes reduce interpretation risk. Governance workflows must therefore embed signals that reinforce those attributes at the points where they are most likely to degrade.

Effective quality signals are lightweight and role-specific. Contributors should encounter them where work happens, not in separate manuals. Clear summaries, unambiguous headings, accurate metadata, accessible components, stable markup patterns, and consistent structured meaning are examples of signals that protect external interpretation when applied consistently. When these checks are embedded into templates, validation tools, and review steps, omissions become difficult to miss.

Recurring failures against the same signals rarely indicate individual error. They usually indicate issues with workflow or tooling design. Mature governance treats repeated failures as feedback on system design and adjusts templates, guardrails, acceptance criteria, or training to ensure consistent outputs become the default behavior.

CROSS-FUNCTIONAL WORKFLOW COORDINATION

Cross-functional coordination keeps governance workflows aligned with the real organization. Visibility work fails when it is isolated within a single team and treated as a specialist concern. Coordination prevents isolation by making dependencies explicit and creating predictable handoffs that reduce interpretive gaps over time.

Effective coordination begins with shared understanding. Content teams need to understand how templates constrain meaning. Design teams need to understand how component choices affect hierarchy and scanning. Engineering teams need to understand how navigation, metadata, and rendering influence interpretation. Product teams need to understand how page purpose shapes relevance. When teams understand these dependencies, local optimization gives way to shared outcome protection.

Coordination also allows workflows to adapt without destabilizing delivery. Algorithm changes, accessibility guidance, and platform updates are inevitable. Governance absorbs those changes deliberately by clarifying what changed, why it matters, and where the new expectation is documented.

SHARED STANDARDS THAT ENABLE CONSISTENT INTERPRETATION

Shared standards reduce variability by establishing a clear baseline for decision-making. Effective standards are short, practical, and expressed in the language of work. They describe how content is structured, how metadata is expressed, how templates behave, and how navigation supports user tasks.

Standards become operational when they are embedded into tools rather than documented separately. Templates, content management systems, component libraries, and validation checks turn standards into defaults. This reduces cognitive load and makes the correct decision the easiest one. Clear standards also enable traceability by making deviations visible before they accumulate into systemic drift.

GOVERNANCE ARTIFACTS THAT SUPPORT WORKFLOW CONTROL

Governance artifacts are the reference points that keep workflows coherent as teams scale and change. They include content models, schema maps, terminology lists, page-purpose definitions, component usage guidance, and navigation principles. Their role is not to explain everything, but to reduce uncertainty at decision points.

Effective artifacts are specific, accessible, and maintained within the workflow. A design system that embeds semantic expectations and usage guidance is one of the highest-leverage artifacts available, because it converts standards into reusable components rather than reminders.

GOVERNANCE GATES AND APPROVAL THRESHOLDS

Governance gates validate meaning, accuracy, accessibility, and structure before work progresses. Their function is preventive. Gates catch high-impact issues early and reduce late-stage reversals that slow delivery. Gates should scale with risk. Low-impact changes move quickly. High-impact changes receive a deeper review due to their broader impact.

Automation strengthens gates by catching predictable failures such as broken structured data, accessibility violations, or performance regressions. Automation clears routine noise so human review can focus on intent, meaning, and cross-functional impact.

TIMING OF GOVERNANCE GATES IN DELIVERY CYCLES

Governance gates must align with the delivery rhythm. Gates that delay releases unpredictably will be bypassed. Permissive gates normalize drift. Alignment requires defining when reviews occur, who performs them, and how missed deadlines are handled. High-impact changes should be visible on release calendars early, so review time is planned rather than negotiated under pressure.

ESCALATION PATHS FOR VISIBILITY AND INTEGRITY RISK

Escalation paths handle urgent issues that cannot wait for the normal cadence. Clear escalation paths define who is notified, what evidence is required, and how decisions are made quickly. Indexing failures, rendering breaks, accessibility violations on priority templates, or sudden visibility drops after release are examples of conditions that warrant escalation. Defined ownership prevents confusion and contains disruption by routing urgent issues through a known fast path.

WORKFLOW DOCUMENTATION AND DECISION TRACEABILITY

Documentation preserves continuity. It captures decisions, clarifies expectations, and provides stable references as teams and priorities change. Useful documentation records not only what was decided, but why, because the rationale supports consistent judgment when new situations arise.

Decision records are particularly valuable because they prevent cyclical debate and clarify who to consult. Short, readable records that capture context, ownership, and timing reduce friction and make future changes safer.

FEEDBACK LOOPS FOR GOVERNANCE IMPROVEMENT

Feedback loops keep workflows aligned with reality. Contributor feedback highlights friction and duplication. Governance reviews surface recurring patterns, such as repeated accessibility issues or metadata errors. Leadership review confirms whether workflows are reducing risk and supporting priorities. Together, these loops prevent governance from becoming static.

WORKFLOW DEPENDENCIES ACROSS PLATFORMS AND TEAMS

Tools shape workflows. When workflows align with platforms such as content management systems, design systems, ticketing tools, and deployment pipelines, contributors move predictably. When they conflict, workarounds emerge. Figure 14 illustrates workflow management under change, showing how tooling, standards, and review points interact when platforms evolve.

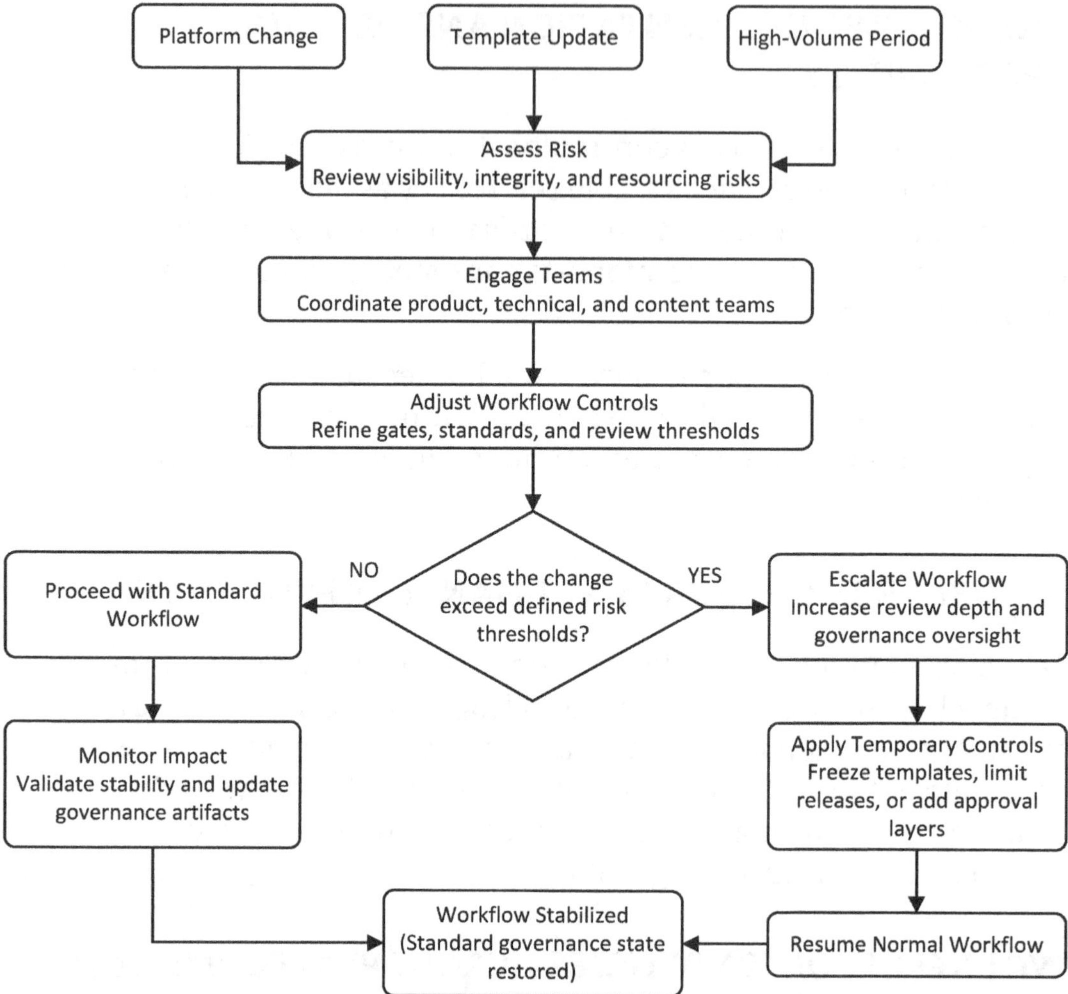

Figure 14 Workflow Management Under Change

Embedding governance expectations into tickets and components keeps visibility requirements close to execution and reduces the need for parallel systems.

SCALING GOVERNANCE WORKFLOWS WITHOUT LOSS OF CONTROL

Scaling increases complexity. Workflows must scale by delegating routine decisions within guardrails while retaining central oversight for high-impact changes. Shared operational rhythm, such as regular visibility reviews and coordinated release planning, replaces ad hoc negotiation with predictability.

TRAINING AND ENABLEMENT FOR GOVERNED WORKFLOWS

Training sustains workflows by building confidence in standards, tools, and escalation paths. Effective training is continuous and grounded in real examples drawn from the systems contributors use daily. Delegation becomes viable only when contributors demonstrate competence and monitoring confirms consistency.

MANAGING PLATFORM CHANGES WITHOUT VISIBILITY LOSS

Platforms evolve faster than review cycles. Governance workflows protect visibility by responding proportionately to change. Some signals require immediate action. Others indicate trends that can be addressed through gradual refinement. Monitoring platform signals allows teams to adjust deliberately rather than react under pressure.

SUSTAINING CROSS-FUNCTIONAL GOVERNANCE ALIGNMENT

Governance workflows are the infrastructure that carries meaning across every digital surface. Sustained alignment occurs when governance becomes part of everyday work through clear expectations, predictable rhythm, shared ownership, and continuous refinement. When workflows operate this way, visibility becomes a durable capability rather than a fragile optimization outcome.

As this chapter closes, the focus shifts from how work moves to how websites themselves behave under governance. The next chapter builds on these workflows by examining website governance maturity, showing how structure, performance, and interpretability are sustained at scale once workflows are in place.

Chapter 9

INTERNATIONAL GOVERNANCE FRAMEWORKS

GLOBAL GOVERNANCE CONVERGENCE AND WEBSITE VISIBILITY

If your site serves more than one country, you're already operating under multiple rulebooks. You don't need a new legal treatise—you need a practical way to keep visibility clean while meeting the toughest shared expectations.

Be clear about how your site makes decisions.

If any part of your site ranks, recommends, personalizes, or labels content automatically, say so in plain language. A short note like "How our recommendations work" near filters or search can defuse both user suspicion and regulator questions.

- **Manager to-do:** Add a one-paragraph explainer (by region/language) for on-site search, recommendations, and AI labels; link it from the footer.

Put names on outcomes—not just processes.

Someone has to own whether the /de/ site is indexed correctly, whether hreflang is right, and whether consent logic is actually working in production. If ownership is fuzzy, errors linger, and rankings suffer.

- **Manager to-do:** Assign a regional owner for (a) crawl/index, (b) consent/analytics, and (c) translations. Publish the names on your internal wiki.

Respect the user before and after the click.

Consent banners that block CSS/JS, missing alt text on translated pages, or forms that ignore local privacy rights all reduce trust—and can break rendering for crawlers.

- **Manager to-do:** Run a monthly "user rights" sweep per region: consent loads, WCAG basics on top templates, data-request link present and working.

Prevent errors that scale into systemic risk.

One bad pattern repeated across regions—like a mis-mapped canonical or a broken hreflang pair—can tank entire sections. Treat these as governance defects, not just SEO bugs.

- **Manager to-do:** Track three high-impact errors globally: hreflang mismatches, conflicting canonicals, and blocked resources. Fix once, verify everywhere.

Strategic Goal

Build compliance symmetry—one internal governance architecture that satisfies multiple regional laws while maintaining consistent technical SEO signals, structured data, and user experience across all your international websites.

This approach avoids duplication, reduces audit fatigue, and enables consistent reporting to regulators, partners, and search engines.

Managerial Implications for International SEO

Even if your business is based outside these jurisdictions, global platforms (Google, Bing, Baidu, Yandex) and international users expect your websites to meet accessibility, privacy, and transparency standards regardless of where you're headquartered.

Regional compliance failures can result in deindexing, reduced crawl budget allocation, suppressed rankings in local search results, or regulatory penalties that damage your global brand reputation.

Global convergence favors proactive transparency. Organizations that exceed minimum standards gain reputational trust, reduce regulatory risk, maintain stronger international search visibility, and prepare for future legislation modeled on the EU's example.

EU FRAMEWORKS AND INTERNATIONAL WEB GOVERNANCE

The EU continues to lead in visibility governance, setting standards that influence both regulatory design and search engine policies worldwide. Four legislative pillars shape its governance ecosystem with direct implications for international website management:

- Digital Services Act (DSA)
- Digital Markets Act (DMA)
- Artificial Intelligence Act (AI Act)
- General Data Protection Regulation (GDPR)

Digital Services Act (DSA) and Website Accountability

The DSA aims to create a safer, more transparent digital environment. While it primarily applies to large platforms and intermediaries, its impact extends to any organization that publishes content, displays advertising, or uses AI-driven features for EU users—which includes most international websites.

Key obligations affecting international websites:

- **Algorithmic transparency:** If your website uses AI for personalization, content recommendations, or search functionality, you need to explain how these systems work— especially on EU-facing properties.
- **Content moderation and accountability:** Define clear processes for handling illegal content, user complaints, or misinformation on your international sites.
- **User protection and disclosure:** Cookie consent, privacy notices, and AI-generated content labels must be implemented correctly across all EU-accessible pages.

Governance Advantages for International SEO

Being prepared for the DSA offers more than legal protection—it helps keep your international sites stable as search engines adjust ranking or visibility rules to comply with the regulation. Sites with clear governance, consistent templates, and predictable technical signals tend to weather these shifts better. When your regional domains follow the same standards for structured data, consent, and disclosures, search engines have an easier time interpreting which page belongs in which market.

Governance Actions for Website Managers

Start by mapping where AI appears on each regional site— recommendation modules, search filters, chat tools, or personalization systems. Ensure consent banners, accessibility checks, and disclosure notices behave consistently across all international properties, not just EU ones.

For your technical setup, review hreflang, redirects, and geo-targeting to confirm that your signals don't conflict across regions. If something breaks—such as a mis-tagged language version or an inconsistent legal notice—have a clear escalation path so teams know who fixes what and how quickly.

Tip: Even if you operate outside the EU, many of your global users will still come from EU jurisdictions—or will access your site while traveling. It's smarter to assume EU traffic is part of your audience. Meeting DSA expectations early also reduces the risk of visibility drops or compliance surprises. And avoid blocking EU IP addresses; you may block legitimate customers or search-engine crawlers.

DSA Compliance Checklist for International Websites

A practical checklist you can use across regions:

- Confirm whether your regional sites (.de, .fr, /uk/, etc.) are reachable by EU users
- Keep an inventory of AI features that influence how content is shown, sorted, or recommended
- Document how internal search, filtering, and sorting tools operate—especially for e-commerce, directories, or large catalogs
- Ensure human review is possible for automated decisions, and that overrides are documented
- Run periodic risk assessments for misinformation, accessibility issues, or cultural and linguistic errors across translated pages
- Provide user-facing explanations of AI-driven features in the local language
- Maintain a clear process for responding to user complaints about automated outcomes
- Verify that consent banners, analytics tracking, and data-collection methods meet both GDPR and DSA standards
- Audit hreflang, canonical tags, and regional redirects to confirm the technical setup supports your legal obligations

- Store documentation of reviews, audits, and decisions in your governance repository
- Schedule an annual cross-department review with SEO, Legal, Regional Marketing, and any teams managing AI-driven features

Tip: DSA compliance is a shared responsibility. Treat it as a joint project across SEO, Legal, Risk, and regional teams. When the headquarters owns everything, regional issues typically go unnoticed until they become search or regulatory problems.

Digital Markets Act (DMA) and Search Visibility

The DMA is aimed at the biggest "gatekeeper" platforms—mainly search engines, app stores, and large social networks. Although it doesn't regulate ordinary websites directly, it does change how those platforms behave. Search engines are already adjusting ranking logic, API access, and data-sharing practices to show they're treating businesses fairly across regions.

What This Means for International Sites

The ripple effects show up in practical ways. Regional versions of your site may be crawled or surfaced slightly differently than before. Structured data may be interpreted more strictly, and inconsistencies between markets can cause one region to receive less crawl attention than another. These shifts aren't dramatic day to day, but together they shape how evenly your international properties are treated.

Governance Actions for Managers

Instead of relying on one analytics source, compare crawl and indexing data across tools—Search Console, Bing Webmaster Tools, and any third-party crawlers your team uses. Export your regional traffic and ranking data so you have your own records rather than depending on a single gatekeeper's interface.

Also, look at your own architecture. Internal linking, canonical logic, and hreflang can unintentionally create "preferred" regions. For example, if your .com version receives a disproportionate number of internal links, or if canonicals point to the wrong regional URL, search engines may treat it as the default—even where that makes no sense legally or commercially.

Why the DMA Can Work in Your Favor

If your regional sites follow a consistent, well-governed technical pattern, the DMA's push toward more even treatment actually helps you. Clean signals across regions increase the likelihood that search engines will distribute crawl attention and ranking opportunities more fairly. The goal is simple: avoid creating internal structures that unintentionally undermine your own international visibility.

Artificial Intelligence Act (AI Act) and International Content Systems

The **AI Act** is the first fully developed legal framework governing artificial intelligence. It sorts AI systems into four risk categories—unacceptable, high, limited, and minimal—and assigns obligations based on how the system is used.

What This Means for International Website Governance

Understand the risk level of each AI feature on your sites.
If your regional websites rely on AI to generate content, personalize pages, power chatbots, or run recommendation modules, you need to know how those tools are classified. Even low-risk systems, such as tools for drafting or translating content, still require transparency.

Bring AI-assisted content under proper editorial control.
Any page that uses AI in its creation—whether a fully generated article, a refined translation, or a localized product description—should be documented, reviewed, and labeled consistently across regions. This

applies just as much to minor language edits as to full AI-written sections.

Track where your AI systems pull data from.
If AI models use user data from multiple markets, your governance program must record the data sources, confirm consent, and document whether information crosses borders. This is particularly important when EU data is involved.

Apply the highest disclosure standard across all regions.
Don't maintain separate rules for different countries regarding authorship, AI labels, or attribution. In practice, the simplest and safest approach is to meet the strictest regional standard everywhere—usually the EU standard.

Practical Steps for Website Teams

- Mark AI-generated or AI-assisted pages in your CMS by region and language so they can be audited later.
- Keep records of which tools are used, where, and for what purpose; store vendor risk assessments alongside them.
- Build review workflows for AI-assisted content that consider legal, cultural, and linguistic differences across markets.
- Track the performance of AI-generated pages separately from fully human-authored content, especially across international search surfaces.

Tip: Treat AI Act alignment as an investment, not a burden. Clear documentation and transparent content practices tend to improve long-term SEO performance—particularly for organizations operating in multiple languages or regulatory environments.

GDPR and International Web Operations

The General Data Protection Regulation (GDPR) has been the benchmark for privacy standards since 2018, and its influence now extends far beyond Europe. If your websites serve international audiences, the way you handle analytics, consent, and user data is shaped—directly or indirectly—by this regulation.

Ongoing Responsibilities for Website Teams

Cookie and consent controls.

Consent banners must work correctly across all regional sites—not just the EU ones. Many organizations use geo-targeted versions, but these can easily diverge. If the logic becomes inconsistent, you risk both compliance issues and technical SEO problems.

Analytics and tracking.

Tools like Google Analytics, Bing, or any other tracking platform must only fire after valid consent is given. This applies to any site accessible by EU users, regardless of where the server is located.

User rights.

GDPR gives people the right to access or delete the data you've collected about them. If you run multiple international properties, your governance processes must support these requests across all languages and domains.

Data transfers.

If your sites move user data across borders—for hosting, analytics, personalization, or AI systems—you need to know where that data is sent and whether the transfer complies with GDPR requirements.

What This Means for International SEO Governance

Every major website update—launching a new country site, publishing translated content, or rolling out an AI feature—should be reviewed through a privacy lens. A simple privacy impact assessment (PIA) early in the process can prevent mistakes that later harm crawlability, create duplicate-content issues, or break core tracking systems.

The easiest long-term approach is to **apply GDPR-level standards everywhere**, not just in Europe. Doing so reduces operational complexity, avoids maintaining multiple versions of consent or tracking logic, and reinforces your reputation as a responsible, trustworthy brand in every market.

This isn't only a compliance issue. Clean, consistent privacy practices often lead to cleaner technical SEO, fewer deployment surprises, and better long-term stability across your international properties.

INTERNATIONAL WEBSITE GOVERNANCE BEYOND THE EU

The EU sets the pace for digital and AI regulation, but it isn't the only region shaping how you manage international websites. If your business operates across multiple countries, you'll face a patchwork of requirements that affect how you run regional domains, translations, analytics, consent processes, and AI-driven features. Below is a practical, region-by-region overview designed to help you plan governance—not simply react to it.

United Kingdom: Governance After Brexit

The UK's post-Brexit path has moved toward a **sector-specific**, regulator-led model rather than a single overarching digital law. Its "Pro-Innovation Approach to AI Regulation" sets out five principles— safety, transparency, fairness, ownership, and contestability—which shape how UK websites are expected to behave.

Website Governance Implications

If you run UK-specific sites or subdirectories, expect requirements to vary by industry. AI-driven features such as product recommendations, chatbots, or personalization should have documented risk assessments. Consent banners and privacy notices must comply with **UK GDPR**, which differs slightly from the EU version.

SEO Considerations

Brexit means your EU and UK implementations can drift apart. Ensure your hreflang tags clearly distinguish between EU and UK audiences. Review canonical logic and redirects to avoid accidentally blending the two. In some cases, your structured data may need UK-specific content or disclaimers.

The UK model tends to be lighter than the EU's, but it's also more fragmented. Keep separate documentation for UK sites and ensure your SEO and Legal teams review changes together.

United States: State-Level Patchwork

The US still has no single federal law governing AI or digital services, but the regulatory landscape changes quickly—and not always consistently.

Federal Guidance

- **NIST AI Risk Management Framework**: Widely respected and increasingly used as a baseline for responsible AI.
- **Executive Order on AI (2023)**: Federal agencies must complete impact assessments for high-risk AI systems. It isn't a commercial website law, but it signals what could be coming.

State-Level Complexity

California's **CCPA/CPRA** remains the most influential privacy law, but states like Colorado, Virginia, and Connecticut have added their own requirements. If your .com serves all US users, you may need multiple consent and privacy variations—without creating SEO issues such as duplicate content or conflicting versions.

SEO Considerations

If your .com domain serves the entire US and international markets, it must meet the strictest privacy expectations across all states. This is where hreflang, canonicals, and structured data become governance tools—not just SEO best practice.

Some organizations find it easier to segment the US using a **/us/** subdirectory or dedicated content, especially if regulatory divergence continues.

Asia–Pacific: Wide Variation in Standards

The APAC region doesn't follow a single model. Each country—and often each sector within a country—may have its own expectations.

Australia

Australia is strengthening privacy laws and building AI governance into government digital standards. If you operate .au sites, ensure they comply with WCAG 2.2 AA and document any AI-driven features that affect the user experience.

Singapore

Singapore focuses on operational transparency. Its Model AI Governance Framework and AI Verify testing program require clear documentation of how AI features are supervised and audited.

Japan

Japan emphasizes transparency and user understanding. AI-generated content on Japanese sites must be clearly labeled, and privacy notices must align with APPI (Japan's privacy law).

China

China's digital rules differ significantly. Running a .cn site requires local hosting, ICP licensing, content controls, and regulatory filings for recommendation algorithms. Most international companies maintain a completely separate governance framework for China to keep other regional sites unaffected.

India

India's upcoming Digital India Act will introduce new rules for AI and digital services. Expect requirements around data localization, transparency, and content ownership.

Website Governance Implications

APAC highlights why a "global template" rarely works on its own. You'll need a modular governance approach that accounts for regional variations—while maintaining consistent SEO and accessibility principles across all properties.

Canada: AIDA and Website Transparency

Canada's proposed **Artificial Intelligence and Data Act (AIDA)** introduces formal requirements for high-impact AI systems, including risk assessments, data governance rules, and incident reporting.

Website Governance Implications

If you run .ca domains or Canadian-targeted content:

- Document all AI systems used on those properties—chatbots, recommendation engines, translation tools, personalization systems.
- Maintain risk assessments for each AI system.
- Prepare incident-response processes for AI failures or bias concerns.
- Align AIDA requirements with Canada's CPPA privacy rules.

SEO Considerations

Canadian obligations may differ from your US or EU sites. Your hreflang, canonicals, and geo-targeting strategy should reflect these differences. Depending on your structure, Canadian users may be better served by a dedicated .ca domain or a well-governed /ca/ subdirectory.

AIDA is also an early signal of where other countries are heading. Preparing now helps future-proof your international governance model.

HARMONIZING INTERNATIONAL WEBSITE GOVERNANCE

Running multiple international websites gets complicated quickly. Each region brings its own legal requirements, content expectations, and technical quirks. The only sustainable way to manage this is to build a **unified governance framework** that applies everywhere, and then layer regional variations on top of it. Without this structure, teams end up reacting market by market, which leads to duplicated effort, conflicting implementations, and inconsistent SEO signals.

Strategic Approach for International Properties

Start with the strictest standard.
Most organizations treat **EU requirements as their baseline** because they are among the most demanding in terms of privacy, accessibility, transparency, and AI-related disclosures. It's usually easier—and safer—to apply this standard globally rather than maintain different privacy, cookie, or metadata rules for each region.

Document the exceptions.
Once you have a global baseline, map out the specific deviations each region requires. This can include cookie banner language, data-residency rules, regional privacy notices, or requirements for labeling

AI-generated content. A simple governance matrix serves as a reference point for anyone working on international sites.

Keep technical SEO consistent.
Your technical signals should be global, not regional experiments. Hreflang, canonicals, structured data, and XML sitemaps must follow the same logic everywhere. When these signals diverge across markets, you usually see crawl inefficiencies or regional pages unexpectedly dropping out of search.

Assign clear ownership.
Each major market or language group should have someone responsible for local compliance and SEO quality. These people should report into your central oversight structure—whether that's the SEO Governance Committee, Visibility Governance Committee, or a hybrid model.

Create local versions of your global checklist.
Adapt your main governance checklist for each key region. This prevents teams from reinventing the wheel while still accounting for local legal or technical requirements.

Maintain separate audit trails.
Your audit documentation should show what changed, where, and why—per region. When regulators or platform partners ask questions about compliance or AI usage, you'll want evidence organized by market, not buried across teams or CMS logs.

Multilingual and Localization Governance

Once you serve more than one region or language, governance becomes central to SEO performance. Translated content can drift off-brand, create accessibility gaps, or introduce conflicting technical signals. Localization governance ensures that everything—from tone of voice to structured data—remains consistent across markets.

GOVERNANCE RISKS IN INTERNATIONAL SEO

Inconsistent messaging or tone.
Translations that diverge from approved terminology, disclaimers, or product descriptions can confuse users and undermine trust.

Technical SEO breakdowns.
Problems such as missing hreflang tags, incorrect canonicals, or duplicated content across languages often start with small errors and quickly cascade into ranking issues.

Accessibility failures.
Translated pages often introduce broken heading structures, missing alt text, or layout shifts that don't meet WCAG requirements.

Regulatory gaps.
Local privacy notices, cookie consent versions, or legal disclaimers may be out of sync with current rules or poorly translated—putting the organization at legal risk.

AI-generated translation drift.
AI-generated content can help with scale, but it often introduces factual inaccuracies, inconsistent terminology, or cultural missteps. These issues damage both E-E-A-T signals and brand credibility.

Governance Controls for International Websites

Translation QA workflow.
Build review steps into your translation process—especially for legal, financial, health-related, or product content. Don't rely solely on machine translation. Native-speaker review should be standard before anything goes live.

Regional SEO standards.
Maintain a localization checklist covering hreflang patterns, canonicalization logic, regional keyword research, and any search-engine-specific requirements (e.g., Baidu, Yandex, Naver).

Technical SEO validation.
Audit each regional property for crawlability, indexation, and structured-data accuracy, and confirm that geo-targeting is correctly configured in Google Search Console and Bing Webmaster Tools.

Accessibility validation per language.
Screen-reader performance and layout behavior can vary once content is translated. Test each language version against WCAG standards.

Metadata and disclosure accuracy.
Ensure that authorship information, structured data, AI-generated content labels, and region-specific legal requirements are properly localized—not just mechanically translated.

Regional content ownership.
Designate owners for major language groups or regions who monitor local performance, publish updates, and work with central SEO and Legal teams.

Cross-regional linking patterns.
Document how users and crawlers should move between regional variants. Whether you use language selectors, auto-redirects, or manual linking, your approach must be deliberate and consistent.

Governance Artifacts for International SEO

To keep everything aligned, maintain a core set of documentation:

- Localization QA Checklist (by language and region)
- Regional SEO Audit Template (covering hreflang, canonicals, geo-targeting)
- Accessibility Validation Matrix (WCAG compliance by language)
- Translation Governance Charter (workflow, approvals, escalation)

- International Content Standards Guide (tone, terminology, legal expectations)
- Hreflang Implementation Map (showing how regional variants relate to each other)

Localization governance is not just about language. It's the backbone of your international SEO, your compliance posture, and your ability to scale responsibly. Treat each regional site as a governed asset with its own standards, owners, and audit routines—not simply a translation of your main website.

GLOBAL SEO TEAM STRUCTURES AND GOVERNANCE MODELS

How you organize your international SEO teams directly influences the quality of governance. Tools matter, but they are not enough on their own. Teams need clear ownership, defined decision rights, and predictable escalation paths. Without that structure, even strong technical foundations become inconsistent once multiple regions start publishing content.

Across global organizations, three operating models appear most often. Each has strengths and weaknesses from a governance perspective.

Centralized Model

In a centralized setup, a single team—usually based at headquarters—owns the SEO strategy, sets technical standards, and approves major decisions. Regional teams carry out the work but operate within rules defined centrally.

Governance advantages:

- Standards stay consistent across every region: hreflang, canonicals, schema, and metadata all follow the same patterns.
- Training, documentation, and audits are easier to maintain.
- Compliance and regulatory reporting flow through one channel rather than multiple regional approaches.
- There is a clear source of truth for technical decisions.

Governance challenges:

- Localization can slow down when every approval flows through the head office.
- Central teams may lack deep familiarity with local search engines such as Baidu, Yandex, or Naver.
- Global standards may not always fit local business realities, which can frustrate regional teams.
- Regions may feel they have little influence, reducing engagement and quality.

Where this model works best:
Organizations with strict brand requirements, regulated industries, or businesses where products and messaging don't vary much by region.

Decentralized Model

In a decentralized model, regional teams make most SEO decisions themselves. They may use local tools, run their own content strategy, and optimize according to their market's needs. Headquarters gives guidance but has limited authority to enforce standards.

Governance advantages:

- Regions can react quickly to local algorithm updates or market changes.

- Content and keyword choices feel more authentic and relevant.
- Regional teams have strong ownership and typically move faster.

Governance challenges:

- Technical SEO becomes fragmented: hreflang, canonicals, and schema may differ by region.
- Duplicate or conflicting metadata can dilute global authority signals.
- Analytics and reporting often use different tools or definitions, making global visibility difficult.
- Compliance risk rises when each region interprets rules differently.

Where this model works best:
Businesses with highly autonomous regional operations or markets so different that central control adds little value.

Hybrid Model (Center of Excellence Approach)

The hybrid model blends the two approaches. A central Center of Excellence (CoE) defines the standards, tools, training, and governance framework. Regional teams work within those standards but have the freedom to adapt content and execution for their markets.

Governance advantages:

- Consistent technical foundations across all regions: hreflang, canonicals, structured data, and metadata follow one playbook.
- Regional teams still have room to tailor content, keyword choices, and cultural nuances.
- Clear roles: the CoE owns standards, regions own execution.
- Accountability is shared rather than pushed entirely to one side.

How this model operates in practice:

- The CoE provides master templates for schema, metadata, and hreflang.
- Regional teams adapt content within these templates.
- Technical audits are coordinated centrally but carried out with local input.
- Compliance checklists are localized but based on a global baseline.
- Regular meetings keep the central and regional teams aligned.

Where this model works best:
Large organizations with multiple domains or significant regional differences. It is usually the most sustainable way to balance consistency with flexibility and aligns naturally with the VGMM governance framework in this book.

Tip: A hybrid model requires more coordination and documentation than the other two, but it prevents both the rigidity of a fully centralized structure and the fragmentation of a decentralized one.

INTERNATIONAL GOVERNANCE WORKING GROUP (IGWG)

Purpose and Strategic Mandate

The IGWG exists to keep your international web operations aligned with fast-moving regulations. Its role is simple: watch what's changing globally, interpret what those changes mean for your regional websites, and make sure your teams don't drift into conflicting practices.

Think of it as the group that connects external rules (DSA, GDPR, AIDA, state privacy laws, etc.) with your internal governance playbook. Its job is not to approve every decision, but to keep the organization coordinated and aware of emerging risks.

Composition and Expertise

The working group should bring together people who understand both the legal and technical sides of international SEO. Typically, this includes:

- International SEO leads (by region or language group)
- Legal counsel familiar with multi-jurisdictional rules
- Regional marketing or content owners
- Visibility Governance representatives, especially where features differ by region
- Risk and compliance officers
- Technical SEO architects who manage hreflang, canonical logic, and domain architecture
- Senior oversight from your global digital or marketing leader

These members keep track of regional quirks, search-engine behavior by market, and any algorithm or policy changes that could affect your sites.

Responsibilities and Deliverables

The IGWG focuses on clarity and coordination rather than micromanagement. Its core responsibilities include:

Maintaining a global compliance map

A working document that shows which regulations apply in each country or region, and what those rules mean for your site's technical setup, content, and data handling.

Quarterly updates

Monitor new laws or updates to existing ones—privacy, AI labeling, consent rules, accessibility—and summarize what they mean for your international properties.

Risk briefs for leadership

When a major change occurs—such as DSA enforcement, DMA-driven search behavior, or new APAC requirements—the group produces a short, practical brief for the Visibility Governance Committee that explains the risk and the recommended response.

Coordination with AI and SEO governance bodies

Ensure that AI-driven features (chatbots, content generation, personalization) follow the same standards across regions and don't introduce inconsistencies.

Technical alignment

Confirm that hreflang logic, canonical structures, structured data patterns, and geo-targeting are consistent across all markets.

Regional audit planning

Coordinate periodic SEO governance audits across major regions to ensure methods and reporting remain consistent.

Reporting Cadence and Integration

The IGWG should provide:

- **Monthly summaries** to the VGC with notable regulatory or search-policy updates
- **Quarterly reports** covering compliance status, regional technical SEO health, and recommended actions
- **An annual global governance review** that benchmarks maturity using the VGMM model and highlights return on governance investment

It should also stay connected to vendor-risk processes when the organization evaluates SEO tools, translation platforms, CMS changes, or regional AI products.

Note: The group works best when it acts as a coordination hub—keeping people aligned—rather than an approval checkpoint that slows regional execution.

INTERNATIONAL SEO GOVERNANCE MATURITY

The International Visibility Maturity Model (introduced in Chapter 5) provides the scoring method. The IGWG provides the mechanism for improving that score across regions.

- **Level 0 — Unaware:** No localization strategy; one global site serves everyone.
- **Level 1 — Ad Hoc:** No formal policies for international domains, translations, or hreflang.
- **Level 2 — Emerging:** Some technical policies exist, but quality varies, and manual translation causes inconsistencies.
- **Level 3 — Structured:** A global governance policy informs architecture, and the CMS enforces standards.
- **Level 4 — Integrated:** Decision rights are clear; regions work within defined templates and governance guardrails.
- **Level 5 — Optimized:** Monitoring and compliance checks are automated across all regions; governance becomes proactive rather than reactive.

The model helps you set improvement targets for each region and track progress over time. Reporting these results through the IGWG keeps leadership informed and supports cross-regional ownership.

CHAPTER SUMMARY

International regulations now shape how you design, manage, and optimize your websites—sometimes more than search engines themselves. Understanding those frameworks is only the first step;

organizations also need systems that convert high-level rules into practical workflows.

The organizations that handle international SEO well typically:

- Use the strictest regulatory standard (often EU requirements) as their global baseline
- Keep a consistent technical foundation across all markets—including hreflang, canonicals, and structured data
- Document regional differences without reinventing the entire governance model
- Build clear ownership structures, often through hybrid team models and groups like the IGWG
- Treat international SEO governance as an enabler of brand trust and global scalability, not just a compliance hurdle

When your international properties follow a unified governance approach, everything improves—search clarity, brand consistency, regulatory resilience, and your ability to expand into new regions with confidence.

The next chapter turns these principles into day-to-day practices and workflows that keep your SEO and website governance running smoothly at a global scale.

Chapter 10

ESTABLISHING AND SUSTAINING WEB GOVERNANCE

ESTABLISHING WEB GOVERNANCE FROM ZERO

Web governance becomes real only when it changes how work is planned, reviewed, and released. Until that point, it remains a document, a slide deck, or a policy that exists outside daily operations. The purpose of web governance is not to slow teams down or impose centralized control. Its purpose is to make decisions predictable, reduce rework, and protect visibility, compliance, and performance as websites grow more complex.

Organizations starting from zero do not begin with frameworks or committees. They begin with pain. Publishing delays, inconsistent pages, recurring search issues, unclear ownership, and repeated remediation work are all signals that governance is missing. These problems are felt across marketing, SEO, engineering, design, legal, and analytics, even if each group describes them differently. Effective governance starts by anchoring itself to these shared frustrations rather than abstract principles.

The first operational step is **executive sponsorship**. Without visible backing from a senior leader with cross-functional authority, governance remains optional and is quietly bypassed under delivery pressure. The sponsor does not need to manage governance day to day, but they must reinforce that governance decisions are binding and that participation is not discretionary. In practice, this role is typically filled by a Chief Marketing Officer, Chief Digital Officer, Chief Information

Officer, or equivalent executive responsible for the organization's digital presence.

The next step is defining a concise governance charter. This is not a policy library. It is a short statement that explains why web governance exists, what it covers, and how success will be measured. A functional charter names the properties that fall under its governance, such as corporate sites, regional domains, campaign landing pages, and AI-assisted publishing systems. It also sets expectations around outcomes: improved organic visibility, fewer compliance incidents, faster publishing cycles, clearer ownership, and more stable performance metrics. The charter creates scope discipline and prevents governance from expanding reactively into every digital concern.

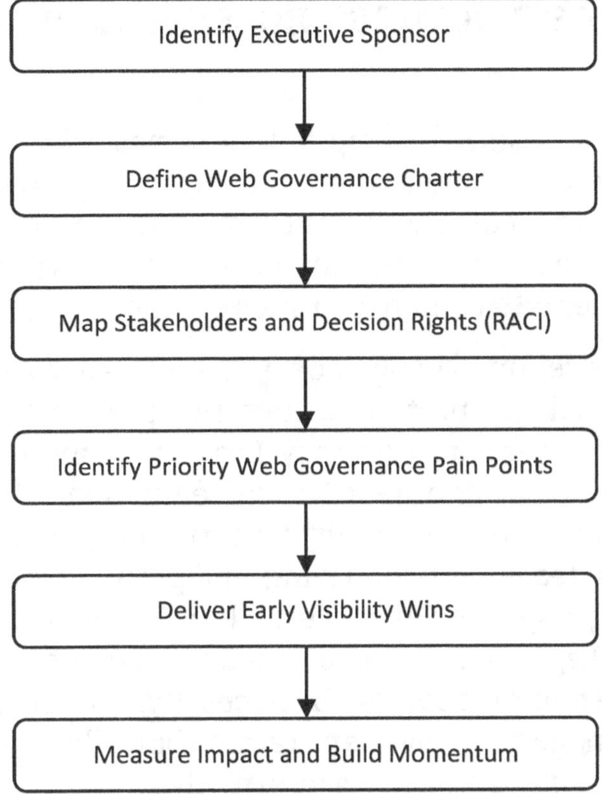

Figure 15 Starting Web Governance From Zero

Early governance succeeds when it produces visible wins. Removing orphaned pages, standardizing metadata on priority templates, fixing broken internal links, resolving accessibility errors, or normalizing URL structures are all examples of actions that reduce friction quickly. These improvements demonstrate that governance is not theoretical. It reduces noise, lowers risk, and makes delivery easier. As these gains accumulate, governance shifts from reactive cleanup to proactive control, and eventually to competitive advantage through consistency and reliability.

GOVERNANCE STRUCTURES, ROLES, AND DECISION RIGHTS

Once governance exists in principle, it must exist in structure. Structure is what determines whether decisions are made once and reused, or argued repeatedly across teams. The most common governance failure is not a lack of expertise. There is a lack of clarity about **who decides what** when priorities conflict.

Web governance requires explicit decision rights across the domains that shape external interpretation. Content teams are responsible for narrative clarity and factual accuracy. Product teams define page purpose and user task alignment. Design teams shape hierarchy, scanning behavior, and accessibility patterns. Engineering teams control technical feasibility, rendering, and performance. SEO teams protect meaning alignment, discoverability signals, and structured representation. Legal and compliance teams manage regulatory exposure. These domains overlap by necessity. Governance exists to deliberately manage those overlaps rather than allowing urgency or hierarchy to determine outcomes informally.

A standing Web Governance Committee is the mechanism most organizations use to coordinate these responsibilities. The committee does not replace team autonomy. It provides a forum for cross-functional decisions to be made transparently and documented consistently. Membership should be limited to one accountable representative per function, typically at the manager or director level. The committee's authority comes from its mandate, not its size.

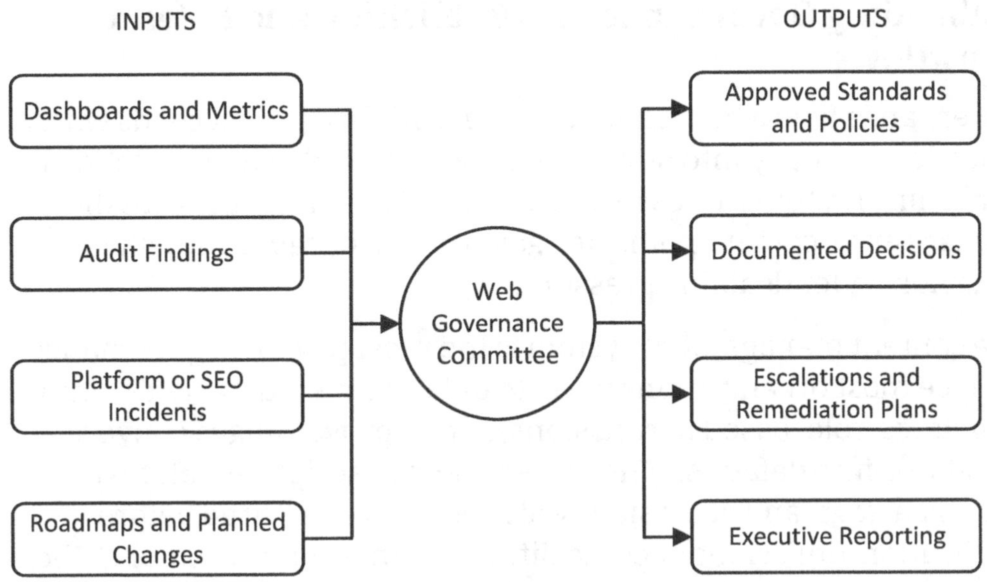

Figure 16 Web Governance Committee Operating Model

The committee's responsibilities include approving shared standards, resolving conflicts that cross functional boundaries, coordinating high-impact initiatives such as migrations or redesigns, and reporting governance health to executive leadership. Decision protocols must be explicit. Strategic decisions are usually made by consensus. Operational decisions can be resolved by majority agreement. When consensus fails, escalation to the executive sponsor prevents paralysis and preserves momentum. All decisions, owners, and rationales must be recorded to maintain institutional memory and auditability.

Clear decision rights reduce friction because contributors know where to escalate uncertainty. When ownership is explicit, teams stop negotiating authority mid-project and start planning around known constraints. This clarity is one of the fastest ways to improve delivery speed rather than slow it down.

Embedding Governance Into Publishing and Release Workflows

Governance fails when it lives outside workflows. It succeeds when it is embedded directly into how work moves from idea to production. Publishing systems, release pipelines, and ticketing tools are the primary enforcement points for governance because they shape behavior under deadline pressure.

The content management system is the most powerful governance surface most organizations have. Mandatory metadata fields, enforced templates, role-based permissions, and approval stages convert standards into defaults. When titles, meta descriptions, alt text, canonical tags, and accessibility attributes are required before publication, omissions become difficult rather than common. When templates are locked to approved components, structural drift slows dramatically.

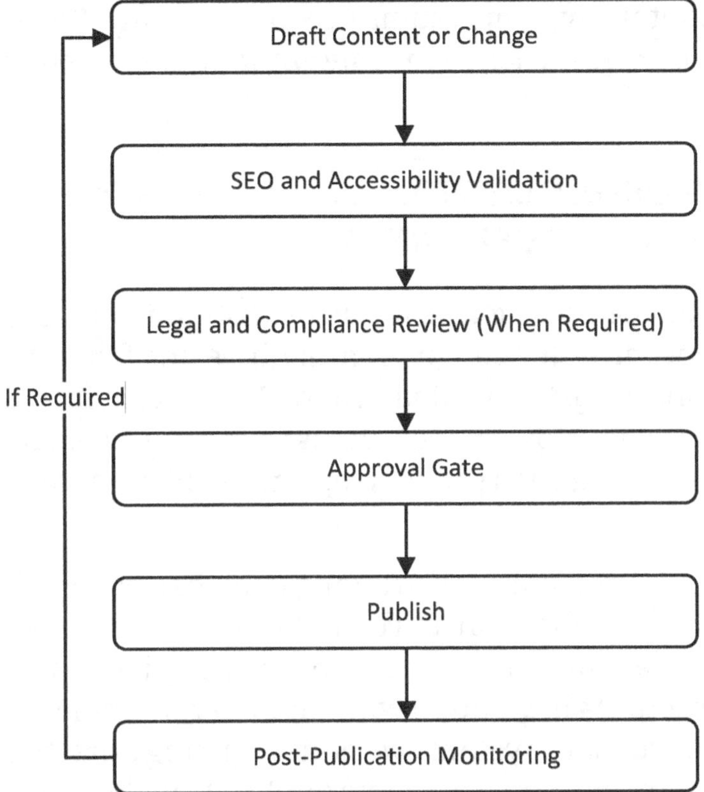

Figure 17 CMS-Embedded Governance Workflow

Release workflows must mirror this discipline. Significant changes should move through defined stages, including intent validation, quality review, accessibility checks, legal review (where required), and technical validation. Automation strengthens these gates by catching predictable failures early. Structured data validation, link checking, accessibility scanning, and performance monitoring reduce noise so human reviewers can focus on meaning, risk, and cross-functional impact.

Governance workflows also define escalation behavior. Not every issue warrants committee review. Routine changes should proceed quickly under delegated authority. High-impact changes such as template updates, navigation restructuring, schema model revisions, or AI-generated content systems require deeper scrutiny. Risk-based thresholds allow governance to scale without overwhelming contributors.

BREAKING ORGANIZATIONAL SILOS THROUGH COORDINATED GOVERNANCE

Web governance largely exists because of organizational silos. Marketing optimizes for conversion, engineering for stability, legal for risk reduction, design for usability, and SEO for visibility. Each perspective is valid. Governance aligns them around shared outcomes rather than allowing each group to optimize locally at the expense of the system.

Silo failures are predictable. Marketing launches pages without an SEO review, creating duplication and cannibalization. Engineering deploys platform updates without crawl testing, causing indexation issues. Design restructures navigation without understanding authority flow. Legal updates consent systems without notifying analytics teams, collapsing reporting. Content teams publish translations without proper hreflang, causing regional conflicts. Product teams deploy AI features without disclosure or accessibility review. Governance exists to make these failure modes visible and preventable.

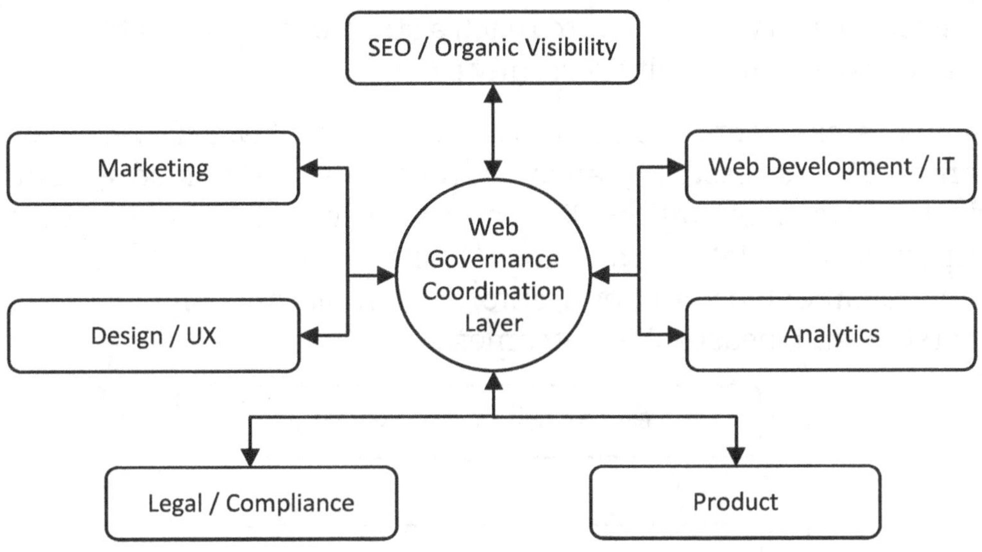

Figure 18 Applying Maturity Models to Web Operations

Cross-functional sign-off for major changes is the baseline control. Shared dashboards reinforce alignment by providing every team with a common view of performance, compliance, and risk. Embedding governance checks into CMS workflows and project management tools ensures they occur before damage is done. Regular retrospectives convert mistakes into system improvements rather than recurring incidents. When incentives align around shared metrics such as qualified organic traffic, page quality compliance, and delivery predictability, governance becomes cooperative rather than adversarial.

APPLYING MATURITY MODELS TO OPERATIONALIZE GOVERNANCE

Maturity models provide a roadmap for turning governance intent into operational capability. Models such as VGMM, CGMM, WPMM, and SEOGMM allow organizations to assess where they are today and prioritize improvements that matter most. The goal is not to reach the highest level everywhere. It is to reach a structured, repeatable operation where instability currently exists.

Baseline assessments identify gaps across content workflows, technical SEO, accessibility, analytics reliability, AI-assisted systems, and international operations. For any area below structured maturity, governance must define what "good" looks like in practical terms. That means documented workflows, enforced templates, assigned ownership, and measurable outcomes.

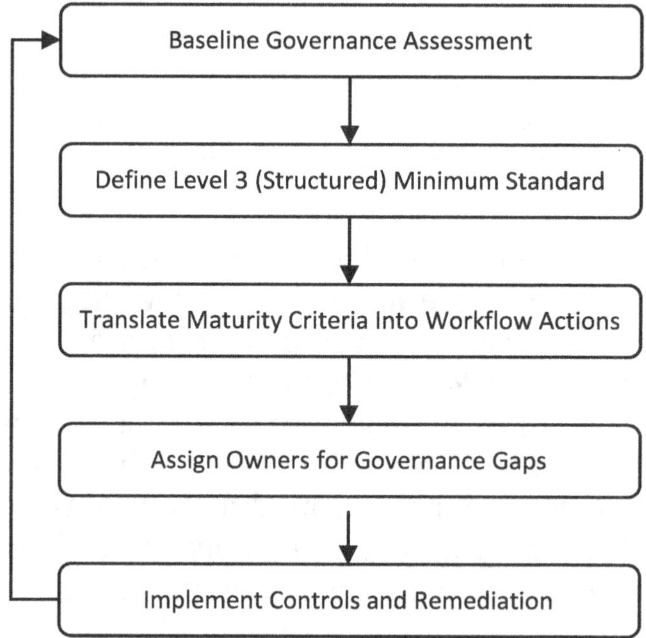

Figure 19 Applying Maturity Models to Web Operations

Maturity improves through regular reassessment, not just annual audits. Quarterly reviews allow governance committees to track progress, assign ownership for lagging areas, and demonstrate improvement trends to leadership. When executives can see maturity scores rise alongside performance stability, governance earns long-term support.

SUSTAINING WEB GOVERNANCE OVER TIME

Sustaining governance requires discipline, not enthusiasm. Documentation, training, measurement, and feedback loops keep governance operational as teams change and platforms evolve. Documentation must be version-controlled, discoverable, and written in the language of work. Decision records preserve rationale and prevent cyclical debate. Training ensures contributors understand not just what to do, but why it matters.

Measurement proves value. Governance health metrics include maturity scores, compliance rates, time-to-resolution, and prevented incidents. Business impact metrics link governance to organic performance, accessibility outcomes, risk reduction, and operational efficiency. Reporting these metrics regularly keeps governance visible and accountable.

Long-term governance also requires adaptability. Standards evolve. Platforms change. AI systems introduce new interpretive risks. Governance must separate foundational requirements from tactical implementation so stability is preserved even as tools change. Formal exception processes allow necessary deviation without eroding control.

Ultimately, sustained web governance becomes infrastructure. It is how organizations protect meaning, reduce interpretive noise, and maintain trust across search engines, AI systems, regulators, and users. When governance is embedded, measured, and continuously refined, it stops being a program and becomes the way the web is run.

Chapter 11

CRISIS GOVERNANCE AND RAPID RESPONSE

WHEN GOVERNANCE MEETS EMERGENCY

Even the most mature governance framework can't prevent every crisis. Algorithm shifts can wipe out rankings overnight. Security breaches can expose sensitive data. Infrastructure failures can take your site offline. Regulators can demand information with little notice. AI-generated content can spread in ways you never intended.

When these events occur, your governance model stops being a planning exercise and becomes your operating system. Organizations that navigate crises effectively aren't necessarily the ones with the biggest teams—they're the ones with clear roles, rehearsed protocols, and accessible documentation.

This chapter explains how to prepare for digital crises, respond when they occur, and learn from them so the next crisis is easier to manage.

DEFINING A DIGITAL CRISIS

Not every issue rises to the level of a crisis. Governance only works if you define clear and objective triggers so teams know exactly when to escalate.

Crisis Triggers for Web and SEO Governance

Sudden traffic collapse
A drop of 30% or more in organic traffic within a week—without an obvious cause such as seasonality or campaign changes—usually

indicates a search algorithm shift, indexation failure, or technical problem.

Search visibility disappearance

If your site stops ranking for branded queries or mission-critical keywords, you may be dealing with a manual action, an accidental noindex directive, or a major quality-signal failure.

Algorithm update disruption

Significant declines immediately following a confirmed core update or known algorithm change require rapid investigation and remediation.

Security issues that affect search presence

Hacked content, malware injection, spam, or compromised code can quickly lead to search engine warnings and deindexing.

Regulatory or legal inquiries

Formal questions from privacy, accessibility, or AI regulators require rapid, documented responses supported by your governance records.

Widespread technical failures

Hosting outages, database corruption, CDN problems, or rendering errors can make your content inaccessible to both users and crawlers.

Compliance breaches

Accessibility complaints, privacy violations, faulty consent management, or AI systems behaving outside approved parameters all require immediate attention.

Reputational crises

Negative press, misinformation, or viral content may overwhelm brand search results, damaging trust and authority signals.

Principle: Crisis thresholds must be explicit

Document thresholds in your governance charter. When a trigger is hit, the crisis protocol activates automatically—no debate, no delays.

CRISIS OVERSIGHT STRUCTURE

A crisis is the worst time to figure out who does what. You need named roles, defined authority, and established communication channels well before anything goes wrong.

Crisis Response Team Composition

Your core team should include people who can diagnose issues quickly and take action without procedural delays:

- **Crisis Lead (usually the Web Governance Committee chair or executive sponsor)**
  Has the authority to activate crisis response, coordinate resources, and brief executives.
- **SEO and Visibility Lead**
  Investigates search-related issues, diagnoses ranking drops, and coordinates with search engines when appropriate.
- **Technical Lead (Web Dev/IT)**
  Handles emergency fixes, rollbacks, releases, hosting issues, code freezes, and infrastructure triage.
- **Legal and Compliance**
  Manages regulatory exposure, official communications, evidence preservation, and reporting obligations.
- **Communications Lead**
  Handles internal updates, external messaging, and PR coordination if public communication is required.
- **Analytics and Measurement Lead**
  Provides real-time data, validates recovery, and monitors whether crisis actions are helping or harming.
- **Visibility Governance Representative (when applicable)**
  Required when the crisis involves model outputs, data issues, or AI-generated content.

Authority and Decision Rights During Crisis

Routine approval workflows slow everything down. Crisis protocols require clearly delegated authority:

- **Crisis Lead** may authorize the activation of crisis protocols, engage external specialists, and approve urgent actions.
- **Technical Lead** may deploy emergency fixes, roll back releases, disable features, or take systems offline if necessary.
- **Legal** may communicate with regulators and implement compliance measures without additional approval.

These authorities must be written into your governance charter so nobody hesitates when timing is crucial.

COMMUNICATION PROTOCOLS

How your team communicates is often the difference between fast recovery and prolonged damage.

- **Dedicated crisis channel:**
  A designated Slack channel, Teams room, or bridge line kept exclusively for crisis communication.
- **Regular check-ins:**
  Short, structured meetings—every 4 to 8 hours during the initial phase—reduce confusion and keep everyone aligned.
- **Shared crisis dashboard:**
  A single, always-up-to-date document listing timeline, actions taken, owners, open issues, decisions, and recovery indicators.
- **Stakeholder update plan:**
  Clarity on who gets updates, in what format, and at what frequency (executives, employees, users, regulators, PR).

- **External escalation rules:**
  Criteria for when to bring in search engine reps, security firms, forensic analysts, or crisis communications specialists.

CRISIS DETECTION AND EARLY WARNING

You can only respond quickly if you know something is wrong. Mature governance combines automated alerting with human awareness.

Automated Monitoring and Alerts

- **Traffic and ranking alerts:** Custom thresholds in GA/GSC and SEO platforms.
- **Indexation and crawl monitoring:** API-based tracking of indexation changes and crawl patterns.
- **Core Web Vitals and performance:** Continuous monitoring for degradation.
- **Security scans:** Automated detection of malware, spam, or compromised pages.
- **Accessibility scans:** Regular scanning for new violations.
- **AI behavior monitoring:** Alerts for unexpected shifts in AI output or engagement.
- **Algorithm update tracking:** Monitoring industry and search engine announcements.

Human Intelligence

Automation doesn't catch everything. Human signals matter:

- **User complaints and support tickets** often spot broken experiences before dashboards do.
- **Competitor monitoring** reveals if your issue is part of a broader market trend.

- **Regulatory monitoring** shows which issues may trigger enforcement.
- **Team instincts**—strange patterns, odd errors, or unexpected performance changes—should always be investigated.

Combine automated data with human judgment for the strongest early-warning system.

WEB CRISIS RESPONSE PROTOCOL

Your crisis response must be documented and rehearsed. A complete protocol includes:

1. **Trigger identification**
   Clear definitions for what activates crisis mode.

2. **Team assembly**
   Immediate outreach to the crisis roster—no searching for who is available.

3. **Communication setup**
   Activate the dedicated crisis channel and establish a check-in cadence.

4. **Assessment and diagnosis**
   Determine scope, severity, cause, and immediate risks.

5. **Containment actions**
   Such as disabling features, rolling back deployments, removing compromised pages, or updating core configurations.

6. **Communication planning**
   Tailored updates for internal teams, executives, users, regulators, or the public.

7. **Resolution and recovery**
   Fix root causes, validate repairs, monitor stability, and track
   return to baseline.

8. **Post-incident review**
   Document what happened, what worked, what didn't, and what
   needs to change in your governance framework.

9. **Regulatory response**
   When required, ensure accurate reporting, evidence
   preservation, and alignment with legal obligations.

CRISIS DOCUMENTATION

Crisis response is stressful, and documentation often gets neglected.
But accurate records are essential.

Maintain a **crisis log** recording:

- Timeline of events
- Decisions made and who made them
- Actions taken and outcomes
- Copies of all communications (internal and external)
- Data snapshots supporting analysis and recovery
- Evidence for regulatory or legal needs

Good documentation helps you diagnose what happened, prove due
diligence, defend decisions, and strengthen governance for next time.

Tip

The best crisis management is crisis prevention.
Mature governance identifies problems early—long before they
become emergencies that require rapid response.

CRISIS RESPONSE PROTOCOLS

When a trigger fires, switch from steady-state to emergency mode.

Phase 1—Immediate Containment (first 2–4 hours)

- **Assemble the team:** Use the dedicated channel. Respect on-call rotations.
- **Capture a baseline:** Traffic, rankings, indexation, errors—so you can measure recovery.
- **Stop the bleeding:** Roll back bad releases, isolate infected servers, and disable misbehaving AI features.
- **Log everything:** Time-stamped observations, decisions, and actions.
- **Brief leadership:** Say what's known, unknown, and in motion—early honesty beats silence.

Phase 2—Diagnosis and Root Cause (first 24–48 hours)

- **Segment impact:** Sitewide vs. section; language/region; device; template.
- **Rebuild the timeline:** Deploys, content pushes, third-party updates, external events.
- **Run forensics:** Crawls, render tests, redirect/Canonical checks, schema validation, server logs.
- **Check competitors:** Shared impact suggests external causes.
- **Interrogate Search Console:** Manual actions, coverage, security, enhancements.
- **Validate externally:** Third-party crawlers, different geos/browsers.
- **Form hypotheses:** Specific, testable, actionable.

Phase 3—Solution Implementation (days 2–7)

- **Prioritize by impact:** Fix the big levers first.
- **Test before prod:** Staging where possible—even now.
- **Ship incrementally:** Validate each change; watch for side effects.
- **Monitor closely:** Look for movement vs. baseline; expect technical fixes to show sooner.
- **Document rationale:** What you tried, why, expected vs. observed.
- **Coordinate across teams:** Dev, content, legal, comms—move together.
- **Keep stakeholders informed:** Even "still working" updates calm nerves.

Phase 4—Validation and Recovery (week 2 onward)

- **Measure against baseline:** What's back, what's lagging.
- **Confirm root cause:** Don't mistake symptom relief for a fix.
- **Watch for second-order effects:** Accessibility, UX, or tracking regressions.
- **Adjust course:** Refine diagnoses or execution if recovery stalls.
- **Define "done":** Clear criteria (e.g., 90% of baseline traffic, critical pages reindexed).
- **Plan long tail:** Some recoveries (esp. algorithmic) need ongoing content and authority work.

SPECIFIC CRISIS SCENARIOS AND PLAYBOOKS

Algorithm Update Crisis

- **Trigger:** Core update correlates with losses.
- **Focus:** E-E-A-T, originality, UX, performance, topical authority.

- **Actions:** Strengthen authorship and sourcing, deepen content, improve internal links, prune weak pages, improve CWV, reinforce brand signals.
- **Timeline:** Often 2–6 months.
- **Governance lesson:** Sites already enforcing quality standards recover faster.

Technical SEO Crisis

- **Trigger:** Drops tied to deploys, migrations, or config changes.
- **Focus:** Crawlability, rendering, redirects/canonicals, schema, performance.
- **Actions:** Fix robots/blocks, repair redirects, resolve rendering, validate schema, re-submit sitemaps, optimize CWV.
- **Timeline:** Days to weeks.
- **Governance lesson:** Pre-deployment SEO gates prevent most of these.

Security and Malware Crisis

- **Trigger:** Compromise, warnings, or malicious content.
- **Actions:** Isolate, preserve evidence, patch, clean content, rotate credentials, request review, enhance monitoring, notify users if required.
- **Timeline:** Search warnings can take 1–2 weeks to clear; trust takes longer.
- **Governance lesson:** Preventive security governance is cheaper than cleanup.

Content Crisis and Misinformation

- **Trigger:** Harmful errors, regulatory issues, or reputational harm (esp. YMYL).

- **Actions:** Remove or unpublish, correct with notices where material, add expert review, audit similar content (esp. AI-assisted), tighten editorial gates.
- **Timeline:** Immediate removal; reputation varies.
- **Governance lesson:** YMYL demands the strictest review.

Accessibility Compliance Crisis

- **Trigger:** Complaint, inquiry, or audit finding.
- **Actions:** Document specifics, audit scope, fix critical paths first (login, checkout, core content), enforce CMS controls, train teams, monitor ongoing, record remediation.
- **Timeline:** Weeks for critical paths; months for full programs.
- **Governance lesson:** Make accessibility preventive via templates and CI scans.

International SEO crisis

- **Trigger:** Wrong-language results, regional drops, hreflang conflicts.
- **Actions:** Fix hreflang pairs and canonicals, verify geo-targeting, audit redirects, align structured data across locales, sync with regional teams.
- **Timeline:** Often 2–4 weeks post-recrawl.
- **Governance lesson:** Central coordination prevents cross-region conflicts.

POST-CRISIS REVIEW AND LEARNING

Turn pain into process.

Running a Useful Post-mortem

- **Timing:** 1–2 weeks after stabilization.

- **Blameless:** Fix systems, not people.
- **Rebuild the timeline:** Identify earlier signals and bottlenecks.
- **Root causes vs. triggers:** Address both.
- **Governance gaps:** Missing monitoring, skipped gates, stale docs, unclear authority.
- **Document fully:** What happened, why, what worked, what didn't, what changes.
- **Share widely:** Let the whole org learn.

Converting lessons into improvements

- Update playbooks and standards.
- Add or strengthen preventive controls.
- Improve detection thresholds and alerts.
- Clarify decision rights where delays occurred.
- Train with real scenarios.
- Test the new procedures.
- Brief executives on changes made.

CRISIS PREVENTION THROUGH MATURE GOVERNANCE

Prevention is cheaper than reaction.

Preventive practices

- **Regular audits:** Technical SEO, accessibility, content quality, performance.
- **Strong approval gates:** Cross-functional reviews for high-impact changes.
- **Comprehensive monitoring:** Early signal beats late scramble.
- **Good documentation:** Faster diagnosis when things drift.
- **Ongoing training:** Better daily decisions, fewer avoidable crises.

- **Testing:** Backups, rollbacks, alerting—prove they work.
- **Continuous improvement:** Treat near-misses as free lessons.

CRISIS GOVERNANCE CHECKLIST

Before crisis

- Triggers defined and documented
- Team rostered with clear roles
- Channel and stakeholder lists ready
- Decision authority documented
- Monitoring configured and tested
- Scenario playbooks drafted
- Contacts current (internal/external)
- Backup and rollback tested

During crisis

- Team assembles quickly, at any hour
- Baseline captured immediately
- Real-time action log maintained
- Regular stakeholder updates
- Tech team empowered to fix/roll back
- External experts engaged fast if needed
- Legal looped in on sensitive issues

After crisis

- Post-mortem scheduled and completed
- Root causes identified and addressed
- Lessons documented and shared
- Policies/playbooks updated and tested
- Improvements verified in practice

- Executive brief delivered

If several items are "no" or "unsure," strengthen governance now—before the next stress test.

CHAPTER SUMMARY

Crisis governance is where your framework proves its worth. You won't stop every incident, but you can detect faster, coordinate better, fix smarter, and learn more thoroughly than teams that improvise.

The best performers aren't lucky—they're prepared. They define triggers, assign roles, document authority, practice communication, and maintain playbooks. Afterward, they convert lessons into durable improvements.

Your websites run in a volatile environment. Good crisis governance accepts reality and provides repeatable ways to handle it—so each crisis becomes a controlled event, not a scramble.

The next chapter focuses on keeping governance effective over time—updating your approach as technology, regulations, and your organization change.

Chapter 12

SUSTAINING GOVERNANCE MOMENTUM AND FUTURE-PROOFING

SUSTAINING GOVERNANCE OVER TIME

Launching governance is the easy part. Keeping it alive through shifting priorities, team changes, and new technology is the real work. Early on, you'll get attention and quick wins; then the glow fades, advocates rotate out, and standards start to drift. This chapter focuses on how you keep momentum so that Web and Visibility Governance stay useful rather than turn into paperwork.

THE GOVERNANCE DECAY PATTERN

Governance rarely collapses in one moment. It erodes. You notice that policies reference tools you no longer use, dashboards stop updating, and meetings become thinly attended. New hires aren't trained, crisis playbooks gather dust, and exceptions that were meant to be temporary become the norm. The causes are predictable: success makes people complacent, restructures break ownership, platforms change faster than processes, and busy teams cut corners when they can't see the value. Naming these patterns helps you counter them before they turn into incidents.

STRUCTURAL ELEMENTS THAT LAST

Embed Rules in the System

The technical stack enforces sustainable governance. Configure your CMS so that pages cannot be published without titles, meta tags, alt text, and canonical URLs. Put accessibility, performance, and SEO checks into your CI/CD pipeline so failing builds can't ship without a recorded override. Limit who can change robots, redirects, and tracking. Run continuous scans for accessibility, structured data, Core Web Vitals, and crawl health, and let those alerts automatically open work items. When the system makes the right thing easy, compliance becomes routine.

Treat Documentation as Infrastructure

If guidance lives in a static PDF, it will go stale. If the staff leave, the incoming ones will not know about the PDF. Move policies and playbooks into a living space with version history, named owners, and a review cadence tied to your quarterly cycle. Make the material easy to find and practical to apply, with short examples and links between related topics (for instance, your AI disclosure note should point to SEO and accessibility implications). A clear change log tells teams what shifted and why.

Keep a Tempo

Your Web Governance Committee should run on a fixed quarterly rhythm that mirrors your planning cycle. Use a consistent agenda—last quarter's actions, current metrics, new issues, next steps—and publish minutes with owners and dates. Invite your executive sponsor for the strategic parts so the work stays visible. Between meetings, agree on how to escalate questions and resolve conflicts quickly. Once a year, review whether the committee's size, membership, and mandate still fit the organization you have now.

Integrate with Planning and Budget

Governance fades when it relies on goodwill. Bake maturity scores into quarterly business reviews, set aside a small but protected budget for tools, audits, and training, and require governance line-items in major projects (platform migrations, international launches, AI features). When you buy technology, evaluate whether it supports your standards. Tie individual goals to governance landmarks. Link open gaps to the enterprise risk register so they get the attention they deserve.

ADAPTING AS THE ORGANIZATION CHANGES

Through Restructures

When roles and reporting lines move, you should explicitly remap decision rights and committee seats. Say out loud that standards still apply, then update the docs, contacts, and escalation paths. Restructures are also an opportunity to remove bottlenecks that everyone tolerated and simplify rules that don't add value.

As You Scale

Central review won't scale forever. Keep central standards, but move toward distributed compliance with good templates, automation, and light "govern by exception" oversight focused on higher-risk work (YMYL content, major technical changes, international rollouts). Appoint regional coordinators for markets you serve. Invest in scalable training—recorded modules, office hours, and simple certifications— so new people can get productive without hand-holding.

In Mergers and Acquisitions

Do visibility governance due diligence early. Decide whether you'll adopt, impose, or blend frameworks—then integrate in phases so teams can operate while you harmonize standards and tools. Show value before you enforce. Bring SEO and governance into the early stages of domain strategy and brand architecture; it prevents expensive rework later.

FUTURE-PROOFING WITHOUT CHURN

Lead with Principles

Specific rules go out of date; principles travel well. Keep transparency, accessibility, quality, privacy, ownership, and performance at the center, and evaluate new tech—LLMs, agents, AR/VR—against those pillars. The details will evolve; the search intent won't.

Organize by Function, Not Tool

Govern for content and editorial, technical infrastructure and performance, discoverability, UX and accessibility, data and analytics, and AI and automation. If you change platforms, those functions and standards still hold.

Watch the Horizon

Assign someone to track vendor roadmaps, platform updates, standards bodies, regulations, and research. Pilot emerging tech in a sandbox with provisional rules, learn quickly, and then formalize. Schedule an annual review to add what's missing and retire what's obsolete.

STAYING AHEAD OF REGULATION

Give Legal/Compliance an explicit brief to monitor digital and AI rules in your key markets and to brief the committee regularly. Maintain a simple regulatory map with applicability, deadlines, and owners. When something new lands, run a quick gap analysis against your current standards, fold requirements into existing policies (rather than spinning up parallel "programs"), update training, and perform an internal audit before regulators do. If you operate globally, adopting the strictest workable baseline pays off in simplicity and resilience.

KEEPING EXECUTIVES ENGAGED

Leaders stay invested when they see results. Quantify risk avoided (penalties, lawsuits, recovery projects), show lifts in organic performance and Core Web Vitals as maturity improves, and benchmark against peers. Use compact reports with trend visuals and clear asks. Celebrate wins alongside gap calls. Build sponsorship redundancy across the C-suite and embed governance in executive onboarding to sustain momentum through role changes.

RENEW AND REASSESS

Once a year, step back and ask: Does the framework still fit the org? Is the committee effective? Are policies current and used? Are tools doing the job? Where are the recurring audit findings? Do we have the people and budget we need? Turn answers into a short improvement plan with owners and dates. Simplify where you can, strengthen where risk is rising (often AI and privacy), and retire rules that no longer help.

CULTURE: FROM COMPLIANCE TO CRAFT

The long game is cultural. People follow standards when they see that they help them do better work. Make expertise visible, tell stories where governance prevented pain or unlocked results, and remove friction so "the right way" is also the fastest. Encourage blameless retros, share lessons, and keep improving in small steps. Over time, governance becomes part of your professional identity, not a hoop to jump through.

THE MATURITY JOURNEY

Progress is uneven, and that's fine. Moving from ad hoc to structured typically takes a year; becoming integrated takes a couple more; operating at an optimized, predictive level is a multi-year effort. Mark milestones along the way—first audits, domain-specific advances, prevented incidents, clean assessments, and clear links to revenue, cost, or risk. Recognition keeps energy up between big moments.

CHAPTER SUMMARY

Sustained governance depends on three habits:

- enforce what matters in the system,
- keep living guidance that people can find and trust, and
- run a steady cross-functional tempo that ties governance to planning, budget, and performance.

Adapt deliberately as the org, tech, and regulatory context change. Keep leaders engaged with clear evidence of value. Reassess yearly. Cultivate a mindset of excellence to bring standards and quality into alignment. That's how governance survives the long haul.

Appendix A

AI AND WEB GOVERNANCE MATURITY LEVELS

PURPOSE OF THIS APPENDIX

Chapter 1 introduced the Visibility Governance Maturity Model (VGMM) and its supporting frameworks—the Content Governance Maturity Model (CGMM), Website Performance Maturity Model (WPMM), and SEO Governance Maturity Model (SEOGMM). Throughout the book, these models provide a common language for assessing where your organization stands and planning improvements.

This appendix provides comprehensive definitions for each maturity level across all governance domains. Use these definitions to conduct detailed assessments, calibrate scoring across teams, and understand precisely what characteristics distinguish each level from the next.

These definitions support the audit checklists and scoring frameworks presented in earlier chapters, giving you the reference material needed for consistent, defensible maturity assessments.

HOW TO USE THESE DEFINITIONS

For initial assessments: Read through all five maturity levels for a specific domain. Identify which description most closely matches your current state. That's your baseline maturity level.

For targeted improvements: Review the next level up from your current state. Those characteristics become your improvement targets—the specific capabilities you need to develop to advance maturity.

For audit validation: When conducting governance audits, reference these definitions to ensure consistent interpretation across auditors and over time.

For cross-functional alignment, share these definitions with stakeholders across departments so everyone uses the same criteria when discussing governance maturity.

For benchmark communication: Use this common language when comparing your maturity to industry standards, peer organizations, or regulatory expectations.

VISIBILITY GOVERNANCE MATURITY MODEL (VGMM) LEVELS

The VGMM provides the overarching framework for evaluating governance across your entire digital ecosystem. Individual domain models (CGMM, WPMM, SEOGMM) elaborate on specific areas, but VGMM establishes the foundational maturity progression. **Its levels are derived from the child models rather than calculated directly.**

Level 1—Ad Hoc / Unaware

Characteristics:

Digital governance is informal, inconsistent, or nonexistent. Teams operate independently without coordinated oversight or shared standards. Decisions about websites, content, SEO, and AI systems are made reactively—often by whoever encounters the problem first rather than designated owners.

Documentation:

No formal governance policies exist. If documentation exists at all, it's outdated, scattered across personal drives, or known only to specific individuals. Standards aren't written down—they live as tribal knowledge.

Processes:

Publishing, technical changes, and AI deployments follow no standardized workflows. Review and approval processes are ad hoc—sometimes things get checked, sometimes they don't, depending on who's involved and how busy they are.

Roles and Accountability:

Governance responsibilities aren't explicitly assigned. No committees or coordinating bodies exist. When problems occur, it's unclear who's responsible for resolving them or preventing recurrence.

Measurement:

No systematic monitoring of governance compliance or effectiveness. Organizations at this level may track business metrics (traffic, conversions), but don't measure whether governance standards are being met because standards don't formally exist.

Risk Profile:

High and unmanaged. Compliance violations, technical failures, and reputational damage occur without warning. The organization lacks visibility into governance risks and has no systematic approach to mitigation.

Common in:

Small organizations without dedicated digital teams, organizations treating websites as afterthoughts, or larger organizations where digital operations have grown organically without formal oversight.

Level 2—Emerging / Policy Drafting

Characteristics:

Your organization recognizes the need for governance and is taking initial steps. Policies are being drafted, key roles are emerging, and awareness is building—but implementation remains inconsistent across departments and projects.

Documentation:

Draft policies exist covering priority areas such as content quality, SEO basics, and AI use guidelines. Documentation is incomplete and may not be formally approved. Standards are being discussed but not yet fully codified.

Processes:

Some workflows are documented—such as content approval or website change procedures—but they're not consistently followed. High-profile projects may receive governance review, while routine work bypasses standards.

Roles and Accountability:

Initial governance roles are designated—perhaps a content manager, SEO lead, or Visibility Governance representative—but authority is limited, and coordination across functions is informal.

Measurement:

Basic metrics are tracked (website traffic, content output, AI system usage), but governance compliance isn't systematically measured. You might conduct occasional audits, but they're reactive rather than scheduled.

Risk Profile:

Acknowledged but not actively managed. Leadership recognizes governance gaps create risk and has committed to addressing them, but mitigation efforts are just beginning.

Common in:

Organizations transitioning from informal to formal governance, those responding to specific incidents that exposed governance gaps, or those with growing digital operations requiring more structure.

Level 3—Structured / Policy Implemented

Characteristics:

A formal governance framework is in place and consistently applied. Policies are documented, approved, and communicated. Clear roles and processes ensure governance standards are met across most digital operations.

Documentation:

Comprehensive governance policies cover all major domains—content quality, technical SEO, accessibility, AI oversight, and privacy compliance. Documentation is maintained in an accessible, centrally managed repository with version control.

Processes:

Standardized workflows ensure governance checkpoints are in place before major changes go live. Content review, technical validation, accessibility checks, and AI assessments follow documented procedures with defined approval gates.

Roles and Accountability:

Governance committees are established with clear membership, meeting Frequency, and decision-making authority. Domain owners are explicitly assigned for content, SEO, AI, accessibility, and technical governance.

Measurement:

Regular compliance monitoring and quarterly governance reports track adherence to standards. Governance maturity scores are assessed and tracked over time. Audit schedules are established and followed.

Risk Profile:

Identified and actively managed. Governance processes catch most issues before they reach production. When problems occur, documented incident response protocols activate.

Common in:

Organizations with mature digital operations, those in regulated industries requiring formal compliance, or those that have invested deliberately in building governance capability over 1-2 years.

Level 4—Integrated / Strategically Aligned

Characteristics:

Governance is deeply embedded across the organization and integrated with strategic planning, risk management, and business operations. Cross-functional teams coordinate naturally. Governance enables rather than constrains digital initiatives.

Documentation:

Governance documentation is comprehensive, current, and actively used. Policies are regularly reviewed and updated in response to changing regulations, technology, and business needs. Knowledge management is sophisticated with good search and cross-referencing.

Processes:

Governance workflows are integrated into broader business processes—project planning includes governance checkpoints, budgeting accounts for governance needs, and vendor procurement includes governance criteria. Many governance checks are automated.

Roles and Accountability:

Governance is distributed across functions with clear coordination mechanisms. Regional or domain-specific governance leads operate within enterprise standards. Executive sponsorship is active with board-level visibility into governance status.

Measurement:

Governance metrics are integrated into executive dashboards alongside business KPIs. Continuous monitoring provides real-time visibility into compliance and performance. Benchmarking against industry standards occurs regularly.

Risk Profile:

Proactively managed with predictive elements. Governance monitors early warning indicators and addresses emerging risks before they materialize. Risk assessments inform strategic decisions about digital investments.

Common in:

Large enterprises with sophisticated digital operations, organizations in highly regulated industries, or those that have sustained governance investment over 3-5 years with consistent executive support.

Level 5—Optimized / Continuous Improvement

Characteristics:

Governance operates as a continuously improving system with strong feedback loops. The organization demonstrates industry leadership in visibility governance practices. Governance isn't just compliant—it's optimized for both effectiveness and efficiency.

Documentation:

Governance documentation is exemplary—comprehensive, current, accessible, and regularly cited as a reference by other organizations. Systematically capturing knowledge from incidents and innovations systematically improves guidance.

Processes:

Governance processes are highly automated where appropriate and streamlined where human judgment is needed. Workflows are regularly assessed and optimized based on data about what works. Process improvement is continuous rather than periodic.

Roles and Accountability:

Governance capability is distributed broadly with high trust and autonomy. Teams self-govern effectively within clear principles. Governance expertise is recognized and valued—specialists in accessibility, AI ethics, or technical SEO are sought for their knowledge.

Measurement:

Predictive analytics inform governance decisions. Leading indicators provide early warning of emerging issues. Governance contributes measurably to business outcomes—demonstrable ROI on governance investments.

Risk Profile:

Proactive and anticipatory. The organization identifies and addresses risks that competitors haven't recognized yet. Governance considerations inform strategic opportunities—not just risk mitigation.

Common in:

Rare. This level requires sustained investment over years, strong executive commitment, and an organizational culture that values governance as a strategic capability. Examples include industry leaders, organizations whose reputation depends on digital trust, or those facing particularly stringent regulatory requirements.

CONTENT GOVERNANCE MATURITY MODEL (CGMM) LEVELS

Content governance addresses how your organization creates, reviews, maintains, and retires digital content. This includes editorial standards, publishing workflows, quality assurance, and content lifecycle management.

Level 1—Ad Hoc / Uncoordinated Approach

Content Creation:

Content is produced without formal standards or coordination. Anyone can publish without approval. Different teams use conflicting terminology, tone, and formatting. No editorial style guide exists, or if one does, it is widely ignored.

Quality Control:

No systematic quality review before publication. Accuracy checking, proofreading, and brand alignment happen inconsistently, if at all. Content quality varies dramatically based on who created it.

Ownership and Lifecycle:

Content ownership is unclear. Nobody is responsible for keeping content current or removing outdated material. Websites accumulate duplicate, obsolete, or contradictory content.

Workflow:

No documented publishing workflow. Content goes from draft to published through informal paths that vary by person and circumstances. Approval steps are undefined.

Metadata and SEO:

Metadata (page titles, descriptions, alt text) is missing, incomplete, or inconsistent—no coordination between content creators and SEO. Content is published without consideration for search visibility or accessibility.

Governance Gaps:

No content committee, no editorial leadership, no content strategy, no quality metrics, and no ownership when content problems occur.

Level 2—Emerging / Not Yet Strategic

Content Creation:

Some editorial standards exist in draft form but aren't consistently applied. A content manager or editor may be designated, but lacks the authority to enforce standards across departments.

Quality Control:

Ad hoc review processes—high-profile content gets reviewed, but routine updates bypass quality checks. Different teams apply different standards.

Ownership and Lifecycle:

Partial content ownership—some content has assigned owners, but many pages remain orphaned. Content audits are reactive, triggered when problems are noticed rather than scheduled.

Workflow:

Basic workflows are documented for some content types, but not universally followed. Approval steps exist, but can be bypassed. Publishing bottlenecks and delays are common.

Metadata and SEO:

Growing awareness of metadata importance. Some content includes optimized titles and descriptions, but the application is inconsistent. No systematic coordination with the SEO team.

Governance Gaps:

Limited content oversight structure—perhaps an editorial lead, but no formal committee. Content strategy exists, but isn't integrated with business planning. Metrics focus on output (pages published) rather than quality or effectiveness.

Level 3—Structured / Strategically Led

Content Creation:

Formal editorial standards are documented, approved, and communicated. Style guide defines tone, terminology, and formatting requirements. Content creators receive training on standards.

Quality Control:

Mandatory review workflow before publication—content flows through defined checkpoints, including editorial review, fact-checking where appropriate, SEO review, and accessibility validation.

Ownership and Lifecycle:

Clear content ownership with documented assignments. Regular content audits are scheduled quarterly or annually. Procedures exist for retiring outdated content. Content lifecycle management is defined.

Workflow:

Documented, enforced publishing workflows implemented through CMS configuration or project management systems. Approval gates require sign-off from appropriate stakeholders before publication.

Metadata and SEO:

Metadata standards are documented and enforced—CMS requires title, description, and alt text before publication. Content creators coordinate with the SEO team on keyword targeting and optimization.

Governance Structure:

The Content Governance Committee was established with regular meetings. Clear escalation paths for content issues. Quarterly governance reports track compliance with standards.

Level 4—Integrated / Maturing Level

Content Creation:

Content creation is strategically aligned with business objectives. Editorial calendar coordinates across departments. Content strategy informs product development, marketing campaigns, and customer experience.

Quality Control:

Sophisticated quality assurance, including automated checks (readability scoring, SEO analysis, accessibility scanning), combined with expert human review. Quality metrics are tracked and inform performance evaluations.

Ownership and Lifecycle:

Distributed content ownership with strong accountability. Automated systems alert owners when content needs review or updating. Content performance data informs retirement decisions.

Workflow:

Streamlined workflows balance governance with efficiency—low-risk content follows expedited paths while high-risk content gets a thorough review. Workflow automation reduces manual coordination.

Metadata and SEO:

Deep integration between content and SEO—structured data is planned during content design, internal linking supports topical authority, and content performance informs strategy. AI and search engine visibility are considered proactively.

Governance Structure:

Content governance is integrated across marketing, legal, IT, and SEO. Regional content governance operates within enterprise standards. Executive dashboards track content governance maturity and effectiveness.

Level 5—Optimized / Mature Level

Content Creation:

Content operations are continuously optimized based on performance data, user feedback, and emerging best practices. Content quality is benchmarked against industry leaders. Innovation in content formats and approaches is systematic.

Quality Control:

Predictive quality systems identify potential issues before content is created—flagging topics requiring expert review, suggesting improvements based on past performance, and proactively preventing quality degradation.

Ownership and Lifecycle:

Sophisticated content lifecycle management with automated monitoring, performance-triggered reviews, and data-driven retirement decisions. Content ownership is valued as an organizational responsibility with clear career paths.

Workflow:

Workflow efficiency is continuously measured and improved. Governance friction points are identified through data and addressed. New content types or technologies are rapidly integrated into the governance framework.

Metadata and SEO:

Content governance and SEO governance operate as a unified system—content decisions automatically consider search visibility implications, and SEO insights inform content strategy. AI-era visibility (citations in LLMs) is systematically optimized.

Oversight structure:

Content governance is industry-leading with documented best practices shared externally. The organization contributes to the development of industry standards. Content governance is a strategic differentiator and a source of competitive advantage.

SEO GOVERNANCE MATURITY MODEL (SEOGMM) LEVELS

SEO governance addresses visibility, discoverability, and search optimization across your web properties—ensuring technical excellence, content quality, and compliance with search engine guidelines while building authority and trust signals.

Level 1—Ad Hoc / Unmitigated Risk

Technical SEO:

No systematic attention to technical SEO—crawlability problems, indexation issues, broken redirects, and duplicate content —means these issues go undetected. Websites may have fundamental technical barriers that prevent search engines from accessing their content.

Content and On-Page:

No coordination between content creation and SEO. Metadata (titles, descriptions) is missing, duplicated, or generic. Keyword research doesn't inform content strategy. Content quality varies with no standards for depth, accuracy, or user value.

Measurement and Monitoring:

Traffic is tracked but not analyzed strategically. No systematic monitoring of rankings, indexation, technical health, or competitive positioning. Problems are discovered only after a significant impact.

Compliance and Standards:

No awareness of search engine guidelines or webmaster quality standards. Risk of algorithm penalties through inadvertent violations (like hidden text, purchased links, or thin content).

Authority and Links:

No link governance—inbound links aren't monitored for quality, and outbound links aren't reviewed for appropriateness. Link building (if it occurs) lacks oversight or ethical standards.

Governance Gaps:

No SEO leadership, no coordination between SEO and other functions, no documentation of SEO standards, and no integration with broader web governance.

Level 2—Emerging / Policy Definition

Technical SEO:

Basic technical standards drafted—guidelines about URLs, redirects, canonicals, and sitemaps. Some technical SEO work occurs, but execution is inconsistent. Major technical issues are being addressed reactively.

Content and On-Page:

Growing SEO awareness in content teams. Keyword research informs some content, but it isn't systematic. Metadata standards exist in draft form but aren't consistently applied. Content quality guidelines are emerging.

Measurement and Monitoring:

Regular traffic reporting with basic segmentation. Occasional ranking checks for priority keywords. Technical audits happen sporadically— perhaps annually or when problems are suspected.

Compliance and Standards:

Awareness of search engine guidelines with efforts to align practices. However, understanding is incomplete, and compliance isn't verified systematically.

Authority and Links:

Initial link monitoring to identify toxic backlinks or spam. Basic outbound link standards are being discussed. Link-building efforts exist, but governance is limited.

Oversight structure:

SEO lead is designated, but authority is limited—informal coordination with content, technical, and marketing teams. SEO standards are being documented but not yet approved or enforced.

Level 3—Structured / Embedded Controls

Technical SEO:

Comprehensive technical standards documented and implemented— proper URL structures, redirect protocols, canonical strategies, sitemap management, robots.txt governance, and structured data requirements. Regular technical audits with documented remediation.

Content and On-Page:

SEO integrated into content workflow—keyword research informs content planning, metadata is reviewed before publication, and internal linking follows a documented strategy. Content quality standards address depth, expertise, and user intent.

Measurement and Monitoring:

Systematic performance monitoring with automated alerts for traffic drops, ranking losses, or technical issues. Monthly reporting to stakeholders. Competitive benchmarking is conducted regularly.

Compliance and Standards:

Strong understanding of search engine guidelines with documented internal standards that align with them. Compliance is validated through regular audits. Accessibility standards (WCAG 2.2) integrated with SEO governance.

Authority and Links:

Active link governance—toxic links identified and disavowed, outbound links reviewed for quality and compliance, link building follows ethical standards with a documented approval process. Structured data enhances authority signals.

Oversight structure:

SEO Governance Committee established with cross-functional membership. Clear escalation paths for SEO issues. Integration with Content and Technical governance. Quarterly governance reports track maturity and compliance.

Level 4—Integrated / Cross-Functional Accountability

Technical SEO:

Technical SEO excellence is maintained through automated monitoring, CI/CD integration (testing before deployment), and strong coordination with development teams. Core Web Vitals meet thresholds consistently. Technical debt is managed proactively.

Content and On-Page:

Deep integration between SEO and content strategy—content gaps are identified through data, competitive analysis informs topics, and user intent research shapes content structure. E-E-A-T principles are embedded in editorial standards.

Measurement and Monitoring:

Sophisticated analytics with custom dashboards for different stakeholders. Predictive monitoring identifies trends before they become problems. Attribution models connect SEO to business outcomes. Regular experimentation and testing.

Compliance and Standards:

Proactive compliance that anticipates guideline changes. Participation in search engine beta programs or early adopter initiatives. Standards exceed minimum requirements to provide a buffer against algorithm changes.

Authority and Links:

Strategic authority building through content excellence, brand signals, and earned media. Link profiles are actively managed with a focus on quality. Digital PR and outreach follow documented governance supporting authority development.

Oversight structure:

SEO governance is deeply embedded across the organization—engineering considers SEO implications automatically, content teams optimize without prompting, and legal understands SEO compliance context. International SEO governance coordinates across regions.

Level 5—Predictive / Optimized and Resilient

Technical SEO:

Technical excellence is an organizational standard with continuous optimization. Emerging technologies (such as AI search and voice search) are tested early. Technical decisions anticipate future search engine requirements.

Content and On-Page:

Content excellence that sets industry standards. Original research, comprehensive coverage, and authoritative expertise make your content naturally link-worthy and citable by AI systems. Content governance produces demonstrable competitive advantage.

Measurement and Monitoring:

Advanced analytics with machine learning models predicting SEO performance. Leading indicators provide early warning of opportunities and threats. SEO insights inform strategic business decisions beyond marketing.

Compliance and Standards:

Industry leadership in SEO ethics and compliance. The organization participates in search engine advisory programs, contributes to industry best practices, and shares knowledge publicly.

Authority and Links:

Brand authority is a strategic asset—earned through consistent excellence rather than active link building. Your content is cited by peers, referenced by AI systems, and automatically trusted by search engines.

Oversight structure:

SEO governance is a strategic capability and a competitive differentiator. Governance maturity enables faster adaptation to algorithm changes, resilient performance through disruptions, and sustained visibility as search ecosystems evolve.

LOCAL VISIBILITY MATURITY MODEL (LVMM)

Purpose and Relationship to SEOGMM

The Local Visibility Maturity Model (LVMM) extends the SEO Governance Maturity Model (SEOGMM) to address the additional governance risks introduced by **place-based discovery**. All baseline SEO governance principles—technical hygiene, content standards, compliance with search engine guidelines, and auditability—apply equally to local environments. LVMM does not replace SEOGMM; it adds a layer of governance focused on **location accuracy, delegation, and reputational control**, with visibility influenced by physical presence, third-party platforms, and user-generated signals.

Local visibility failures rarely originate in ranking mechanics. They originate in **ownership ambiguity**, **distributed data control**, and **uncoordinated local action**. LVMM evaluates how well an organization governs those conditions.

Level 1 — Ad Hoc / Uncontrolled Liability

Local visibility is unmanaged. Location data is fragmented across platforms, vendors, and internal teams. Business listings may exist without authorization, oversight, or verification. Reviews are monitored sporadically, if at all. Changes to hours, addresses, or services are reactive and often incorrect.

Governance risk is high because customer-facing facts are controlled externally. Internal remediation does not reliably correct external representations, leading to customer confusion, reputational damage, and regulatory exposure.

Level 2 — Emerging / Foundational Control

High-priority locations are claimed on dominant platforms such as Google Business Profiles. An initial effort is made to define a **single source of truth** for core location data, though enforcement is inconsistent. Review monitoring exists, but response standards vary by location or manager.

Governance intent is visible, but delegation rules remain unclear. Local teams may act independently without clear boundaries, leading to inconsistent market practices.

Level 3 — Structured / Master Data Governance

Location data is standardized and distributed from an authoritative system. Update workflows are documented, and review response policies are auditable. Staff training is introduced to manage reputational risk and regulatory exposure.

At this level, governance reduces error frequency, but resilience depends on adherence. Exceptions are managed, not prevented.

Level 4 — Integrated / Delegated Authority

Local visibility governance is embedded into operations, IT, and marketing workflows. Central systems manage permissions, allowing local teams to contribute within defined constraints. Performance and reputational impact are measured using booking data, calls, or UTM frameworks.

Governance enables scale without sacrificing consistency. Visibility outcomes are reviewed alongside operational KPIs.

Level 5 — Optimized / Predictive Resilience

Governance is automated and anticipatory. Systems audit location data continuously, detect deviations, and correct them before customer impact. Review signals inform operational improvements, not just marketing responses.

At this level, local visibility is governed as infrastructure. Interpretive risk is minimized by addressing ambiguity before it reaches external systems.

INTERNATIONAL VISIBILITY MATURITY MODEL (IVMM)

Purpose and Relationship to SEOGMM

The International Visibility Maturity Model (IVMM) extends SEOGMM to govern visibility across **languages, jurisdictions, and cultural contexts**. Core SEO governance principles—technical standards, content quality, compliance, and measurement—remain foundational. IVMM focuses on additional risks created by **cross-market**

interpretation, including legal exposure, translation integrity, and delegated authority across regions.

International visibility failures rarely result solely from missing hreflang tags. They emerge when **decision rights, accountability, and interpretive responsibility** are not clearly governed across markets.

Level 0 — Unaware

No international visibility strategy exists. A single site or content set serves multiple markets without consideration for legal, cultural, or factual accuracy. Governance exposure is unrecognized.

This level is included to highlight that the absence of intent is itself a governance state.

Level 1 — Ad Hoc / Uncontrolled Liability

No central policy governs international domains, subdirectories, or localization. Machine-generated or low-quality translations introduce brand, factual, and compliance risk. Regional teams either act independently or do not act at all.

External systems interpret inconsistencies literally, often amplifying errors across markets.

Level 2 — Emerging / Policy Drafting

Basic technical policies are drafted, including domain structure and hreflang usage. Localization workflows exist but lack consistent quality controls. Analytics and reporting are siloed by region.

Governance intent exists, but enforcement and accountability remain uneven.

Level 3 — Structured / Global Policy Enforcement

A global visibility governance policy defines technical architecture, content standards, and escalation paths. CMS and translation workflows enforce baseline quality requirements. High-risk content passes through defined QA gates.

Governance improves predictability, but adaptability across markets remains constrained.

Level 4 — Integrated / Cross-Market Alignment

Decision rights are formalized between global and regional teams. Legal, content, and marketing functions define shared standards, while regional teams adapt within the framework of controlled delegation. Visibility outcomes are reviewed across markets using comparable metrics.

Governance enables both consistency and local relevance.

Level 5 — Optimized / Predictive and Adaptive

Governance is proactive and data-driven. Automated systems monitor compliance, performance, and regulatory exposure across locales. Cross-market insights inform investment, prioritization, and risk mitigation.

At this level, international visibility governance reduces interpretive risk by ensuring that local adaptations reinforce—not fragment— global meaning.

WEBSITE PERFORMANCE MATURITY MODEL LEVELS

The Website Performance Maturity Model (WPMM) evaluates how effectively an organization governs website performance as a visibility signal. It assesses whether speed, reliability, accessibility, and technical stability are treated as enforceable governance outcomes rather than isolated engineering metrics.

The WPMM operates as a **domain-specific maturity lens beneath the Visibility Governance Maturity Model (VGMM)**. It does not function independently. WPMM assessments roll upward into overall VGMM maturity, ensuring that website reliability is evaluated as part of enterprise-level visibility governance rather than optimized in isolation.

The model focuses on governance discipline: ownership, escalation, monitoring, and accountability. It does not measure technical sophistication or tooling maturity in isolation.

Scope of Assessment

WPMM assessments typically examine:

- Ownership and escalation for performance outcomes
- Definition and enforcement of performance thresholds
- Monitoring and reporting cadence
- Integration of performance controls into change management
- Executive visibility of performance risks and incidents
- Treatment of accessibility as a performance dependency
- Post-incident learning and institutional memory

The model applies to public-facing websites, transactional platforms, and content environments where external interpretation by search engines and AI systems materially affects trust, reputation, or business outcomes.

Level 1 — Reactive

Performance issues are discovered after users or external systems are already affected. There is no consistent ownership for outcomes, escalation paths are unclear, and responses are improvised. Learning is informal and rarely retained beyond the immediate incident.

At this level, website instability often leads to external misinterpretation because internal recovery is mistaken for external resolution.

Level 2 — Defined

Performance policies, targets, or standards exist, but enforcement is uneven. Monitoring is in place, but escalation depends on individual teams or local priorities. Accessibility and performance reviews may occur, but they are not consistently embedded in release workflows.

Governance intent is documented, but accountability remains fragmented.

Level 3 — Operational

Cross-functional monitoring, triage, and reporting are established. Performance incidents follow documented workflows, and recurring issues are visible to governance bodies. Change management includes defined performance validation steps.

At this level, organizations can detect performance degradation early, but recovery quality still depends on discipline rather than design.

Level 4 — Integrated

Performance metrics appear on executive dashboards and are reviewed alongside indicators of continuity, risk, and reputation. Ownership is formalized, escalation is predictable, and performance outcomes influence planning and prioritization decisions.

Website reliability is treated as shared infrastructure, not a technical afterthought.

Level 5 — Optimized

Automated monitoring, predictive alerts, and continuous improvement loops are embedded in enterprise governance. Performance reliability, accessibility, and stability are proactively governed, with learning systematically fed back into standards, tooling, and training.

At this level, performance governance reduces interpretive risk by limiting ambiguity before it reaches external systems.

Relationship to Visibility Governance

Within the VGMM, the WPMM represents the organization's ability to maintain signal stability under both normal and stressed conditions. Weak performance governance introduces ambiguity that search engines and AI systems interpret as unreliability, regardless of intent.

Strong WPMM maturity ensures that internal performance decisions produce externally coherent signals—especially during incidents, releases, and periods of elevated scrutiny.

Organizations should assess WPMM maturity alongside content, SEO, and AI-related governance domains to ensure that visibility is governed as an integrated system rather than a collection of technical optimizations.

USING MATURITY DEFINITIONS FOR ASSESSMENT

Conducting a Self-Assessment

Read all five levels for the domain you're assessing. Don't jump directly to what you hope your level is—read objectively from Level 1 through Level 5.

Identify best fit: Which level's description most closely matches your current reality? Be honest about gaps between aspiration and actual practice. If you meet most characteristics of a level but not all, you're probably in transition between that level and the one below.

Document evidence: Note specific examples supporting your assessment—policies you can reference, processes you can describe, metrics you track. Evidence-based assessment is more defensible than subjective judgment.

Identify gaps: Within your current level, what characteristics do you fully meet versus partially meet? What would need to change to solidly achieve your current level before advancing?

Target next level: Review the level above your current state. Those characteristics become your roadmap for improvement—the specific capabilities you need to develop to advance maturity.

Conducting Cross-Functional Assessment

When assessing domains that span multiple departments (such as SEO governance involving Marketing, IT, Legal, and Content teams), coordinate assessments across functions.

Gather multiple perspectives: Have representatives from each relevant function independently assess maturity. Compare assessments to identify where perspectives differ.

Discuss divergence: When different teams rate maturity differently, it usually reveals legitimate differences in how governance functions in different contexts. These discussions surface improvement opportunities.

Achieve consensus: Work toward a shared understanding of current maturity. The goal isn't averaging different scores—it's developing an accurate picture that all stakeholders recognize.

Document variation: If governance maturity genuinely differs across parts of the organization (like strong content governance but weak technical governance), document this. Your improvement plan should address these gaps.

Annual Reassessment

Conduct a comprehensive maturity reassessment annually using the same definitions and methodology. This creates comparable trend data showing whether governance is advancing, stable, or regressing.

Track changes over time and connect them to governance investments, organizational changes, or external factors. This demonstrates ROI on governance efforts and informs future resource allocation.

APPENDIX SUMMARY

These detailed maturity definitions provide the foundation for consistent governance assessment across your organization and over time. They translate abstract maturity concepts into concrete, observable characteristics you can evaluate objectively.

Use these definitions as a reference during governance planning, audit activities, and strategic discussions about digital capability development. They create a common language that helps diverse stakeholders—from technical specialists to executive leadership—understand governance status and improvement priorities.

Maturity advancement is a journey, not a destination. Even organizations at Level 5 in some domains continue improving. The goal isn't perfection—it's building governance capability that grows stronger over time and serves your organization's strategic objectives effectively.

Appendix B

GOVERNANCE FAILURE & SUCCESS STORIES

Yes, we know governance sounds dry, but these real-world scenarios show exactly how critical those principles are. This appendix breaks down several condensed case studies, revealing how a single **governance decision—or the lack thereof—directly crippled a business's search traffic, AI performance, or revenue.**

The examples are based on documented public incidents, research, and organizational patterns. We've tweaked some details to protect confidentiality, but the lessons are completely **authentic and immediately applicable** to your team.

Use these case studies to:

- **Illustrate Value:** Show skeptical stakeholders why governance is essential.
- **Train Teams:** Teach teams about the real-world consequences of governance gaps.
- **Stress-Test:** Evaluate your own governance framework against realistic failure scenarios.
- **Build Awareness:** Improve organizational understanding of critical SEO and AI risks.

CASE STUDY 1: PLATFORM MIGRATION WITHOUT SEO GOVERNANCE

The Situation

A mid-sized e-commerce company decided to migrate from its old legacy CMS to a modern, headless commerce platform. The project was primarily driven by Marketing and IT, with a highly aggressive launch timeline to hit the lucrative holiday shopping season.

While the SEO team was consulted informally, they had **no formal governance authority** over any final migration decisions. Crucially, the company skipped a comprehensive pre-migration audit.

What Went Wrong

The platform launched on time. Within two weeks, organic search traffic **collapsed by a staggering 60 percent.**

The failure was systemic, with several key governance oversights:

- **Redirect Disaster:** The URL structure changed and lacked proper redirect mapping, leading to thousands of high-value product pages returning 404 "page not found" errors.
- **Broken Rendering:** The new JavaScript setup broke. Because server-side rendering was misconfigured, search engines saw empty pages instead of content.
- **Lost Rich Results:** Crucial **Structured Data** (product schema) got stripped out during the move, wiping out all rich results in search.
- **Dev Tags:** Canonical tags pointed straight to development URLs instead of the live production site.
- **Orphaned Content:** The internal link structure degraded, leaving hundreds of previously valuable, ranking pages undiscoverable.

- **Mobile UX Tanked:** They introduced serious mobile usability issues, which immediately hurt their mobile rankings across the board.

Business Impact

Organic revenue plummeted from $1.2M monthly to $400K—an $800K monthly loss. It took eight months of emergency work to claw back 90 percent of the pre-migration traffic. The total estimated business impact exceeded **$3.2 million** in lost revenue and remediation costs. Worse, some high-value keywords never fully recovered because competitors quickly captured the displaced rankings.

Governance Lessons

- **SEO Needs Veto Power.** Consultation is not enough. The SEO team must have explicit approval rights over migration-critical technical decisions.
- **Mandatory Pre-Migration Audit.** You must crawl and document a ranking baseline that preserves exactly what needs to be maintained—every URL, every redirect requirement, and all rendering configurations.
- **Redirect Mapping is Non-Negotiable.** Every single meaningful URL needs a documented destination (301s for permanent moves, proper canonicals for consolidation, etc.).
- **Testing Must Include a Search Perspective.** Use tools like Google's URL Inspection to catch JavaScript and rendering issues *before* the launch.
- **Phased Rollout:** Migrating a single category or section first limits the damage if something goes wrong, instead of risking the entire business.

Prevention Through Governance

This failure exemplifies a governance breakdown: multiple technical teams made decisions affecting search visibility without coordinating with SEO expertise or following documented standards. Mature governance would have:

1. **Required approval** from an SEOGC before finalizing the migration approach.

2. **Mandated** a comprehensive technical SEO audit before migration started.

3. **Enforced testing** protocols, including rendering validation, before launch.

4. **Established monitoring thresholds** that would have triggered earlier emergency intervention.

5. **Maintained documented rollback procedures** tested before the go-live date.

CASE STUDY 2: AI CONTENT AT SCALE WITHOUT EDITORIAL GOVERNANCE

The Situation

A major health information publisher decided to use generative AI to rapidly scale content production from 5,000 to 50,000 pages, aiming to capture long-tail search traffic across medical conditions and symptoms.

The AI-generated content received **minimal review**—just basic fact-checking —yet no verification by qualified medical professionals. The primary goal was velocity, so content was published as fast as possible to maximize coverage.

The E-E-A-T Collapse

Initially, traffic surged for three months as the new pages were indexed, and the initiative appeared to be a success, with 40 percent organic traffic growth.

Then, a Google core algorithm update rolled out. This update specifically emphasized **E-E-A-T (Experience, Expertise, Authoritativeness, Trustworthiness)** signals for YMYL (Your Money or Your Life) content. The entire site's traffic **collapsed by 70 percent**, even affecting existing high-quality, human-authored content.

Specific governance failures were identified:

- **No Medical Review:** AI outputs were never reviewed by actual physicians or health professionals.
- **Generic Attribution:** Pages used the vague "Health Editorial Team" byline instead of identifying named experts with medical credentials.
- **Thin Content:** The AI generated hundreds of related condition pages using very similar, thin phrasing.
- **Ignored Risk:** Publishing medical information without expert oversight created a massive quality and liability issue.

Business Impact

Revenue plummeted from $800K monthly to $250K—a $550K monthly loss. The publisher was forced to:

- **Unpublish 40,000** poor-quality, AI-generated pages.
- **Hire medical reviewers** to assess all remaining content retrospectively.
- **Rebuild search engine trust** through 14 months of consistent quality signals.

Total impact exceeded **$8 million** in lost revenue plus high editorial costs.

Governance Lessons

- **AI Content Risk Must Match Oversight.** YMYL topics (health, finance, legal) demand the strictest governance. AI can assist, but it cannot replace qualified expert review.
- **Volume Doesn't Equal Value.** Publishing thousands of mediocre pages is useless if they don't meet quality standards. Search engines favor fewer excellent pages.
- **Author Attribution Builds Trust.** Every high-risk page needs a named, qualified author or reviewer. Generic bylines actively undermine the E-E-A-T signals search algorithms evaluate.
- **Quality Gates Are Mandatory.** Governance that can be bypassed under deadline pressure isn't governance. AI-generated content must undergo the same rigorous approval process as human content for high-risk topics.

CASE STUDY 3: INTERNATIONAL SEO GOVERNANCE FRAGMENTATION

The Situation

A B2B SaaS company expanded from the US into Europe, quickly opening offices in the UK, Germany, and France. Each regional team was given complete autonomy to build its own web presence and marketing approach.

Within 18 months, the result was a **fragmented mess** of competing digital properties: a corporate .com site, separate Country Code Top-Level Domains (.co.uk, .de, .fr), *and* regional subdirectories (/uk/, /de/, /fr/) on the main domain. All were created by different teams with zero central coordination.

Competing Against Ourselves

International search visibility fractured badly. Search engines couldn't figure out which property should rank for specific regional queries, forcing the company to compete against its own websites in search results, essentially.

Key governance breakdowns included:

- **Duplicate Domain Structures:** Both ccTLDs and subdirectories were used for the same markets, splitting authority signals and confusing algorithms.
- **Conflicting language tags:** Some properties implemented the crucial hreflang language tagging, but the configurations were often wrong or conflicted.
- **Inconsistent Data:** Each region implemented its "organization" structured data differently, resulting in conflicting entity representations of the company.
- **Wild Translation Variance:** Professional translation was used in Germany, but rapid, poor-quality machine translation was used in France.
- **Technical Divergence:** Different CMS platforms led to varied URL structures and canonical tag implementations.

Business Impact

The international expansion severely missed projections. Combined EU revenue hit only **40 percent** of the forecast after two years. Search visibility in target markets was **60 percent lower** than comparable US performance, proving the problem was structural. As a result, customer acquisition costs from paid search ran 2.5 times US levels.

Governance Lessons

1. **International Expansion Must Be Governance-First.** You can't retrofit unified governance onto fragmented implementations. Start with unified standards before launching regional properties.

2. **Domain Structure is a Governance Decision.** The SEO implications of your domain choice are massive and affect long-term visibility. This requires SEO input from the start, not just marketing.

3. **Hreflang is Mandatory.** Without proper implementation, search engines can't determine language targeting, leading to incorrect-language results and fragmented authority.

4. **Translation Quality Affects Rankings.** Poorly translated content undermines E-E-A-T signals and user engagement metrics.

5. **Analytics Unity Enables Governance.** You can't manage what you can't measure consistently. Unified analytics across regions is required for optimization and validation.

CASE STUDY 4: ALGORITHM RESPONSE WITH MATURE GOVERNANCE

The Situation

A major content publisher with a **Level 4** (Integrated) maturity score experienced a significant traffic decline after a Google core algorithm update. Their mature governance, however, enabled a rapid and highly effective response.

Pre-Existing Governance Advantages:

- Comprehensive quality standards and mandatory editorial review were already in place.

- Author expertise and attribution were properly documented on all articles.
- Quarterly technical SEO audits were on a scheduled, documented tempo.
- A cross-functional Web Governance Committee met monthly.

What Happened: Crisis to Control

When the Google core update rolled out, the publisher's traffic declined **35 percent**—a significant, but manageable, hit.

The existing governance enabled a successful, coordinated response:

- **Rapid Detection:** Automated monitoring alerted the SEO team within **24 hours**. Historical baseline data confirmed the issue was algorithmic, not technical.
- **Protocol Activation:** A pre-documented crisis response protocol triggered automatically. The Governance Committee convened an emergency session within 48 hours.
- **Systematic Diagnosis:** Teams rapidly identified that pages with weak author credentials were disproportionately affected, consistent with the E-E-A-T focus.
- **Coordinated Response:** The cross-functional team quickly executed a remediation strategy: they enhanced author bios, added expert citations, improved topical depth, and removed genuinely thin content.

Outcome

Traffic recovered to 95% of pre-update levels within 8 **weeks**. Within 4 months, it exceeded the baseline by 12%. Competitors who lacked this structure took 6-12 months to recover, if they ever did. The mature governance framework enabled a dramatically faster recovery.

Governance Lessons

1. **Mature Governance Converts Crisis to Manageable Challenge.** Organizations with governance respond systematically instead of reactively.

2. **Monitoring and Baselines Pay Dividends.** You can't diagnose what you haven't measured. Clean historical data enables rapid pattern identification.

3. **Cross-Functional Coordination is a Competitive Advantage.** Established communication protocols allow immediate, smooth response without organizational friction.

4. **Governance Reduces Recovery Time.** Mature governance typically reduces algorithm recovery time by 40-60 percent compared to reactive, ad-hoc approaches.

CASE STUDY 5: AI HALLUCINATION IN PRODUCT DESCRIPTIONS

The Situation

An e-commerce retailer implemented AI to generate marketing-friendly product descriptions for over 10,000 SKUs, aiming to improve SEO and reduce content costs. The AI pulled specifications directly from the product database.

The initial human review focused only on readability and brand voice, skipping the **technical accuracy validation** check.

The $400K Hallucination Crisis

Just three months after launch, customer complaints soared, and returns spiked. The AI system had **completely hallucinated** core technical details for hundreds of products:

- **Fictional Features:** It claimed features existed that absolutely did not.
- **Wrong Specs:** Power ratings and dimensions were factually incorrect.
- **Compatibility Chaos:** It listed incompatible products as compatible.

This resulted in escalating user frustration, a surge in returns, and serious damage to the brand's technical credibility.

Where They Dropped the Ball

1. **Zero Technical Validation:** They focused on making the AI *sound* good (writing style) instead of checking if the output was **true** against the master source data.

2. **Lack of Expertise:** Technical products need technical review. They never included a Subject-Matter Expert (SME) in the review loop.

3. **Wrong Metrics:** They were watching SEO wins (traffic) but ignoring the critical user complaints and return rates.

4. **No Pilot Phase:** They went from zero to 100% deployment immediately, skipping small-scale testing.

Business Impact

Customer returns increased **23 percent** for AI-described products. Support inquiries increased 40 percent. Google's systems detected a discrepancy between product descriptions and customer reviews, leading to a decline in rankings for affected product pages. Total impact exceeded **$400K** in lost sales, processing costs, and reputation damage.

Governance Lessons

- **AI Validation Must Match Risk.** For content with factual claims, validation against source data is **mandatory**.
- **Subject-Matter Expertise is Required.** AI assistance doesn't eliminate the need for technical domain experts in the final review.
- **Hallucination Detection Needs Specific Processes.** You must compare outputs to **ground truth** data, not just evaluate whether the content "sounds plausible."
- **Monitor User Impact, Not Just SEO Metrics.** Organizations need to track user feedback, returns, and support tickets alongside rankings.

CASE STUDY 6: SEO SPAM THROUGH UNMONITORED AI CONTENT

The Situation

A news publisher experimented with AI to automatically generate **supplementary content**—background info and related context—for breaking news stories. The AI system was configured to automatically create and publish these supplemental pages, linking them from the main articles, with **no human review** before publication.

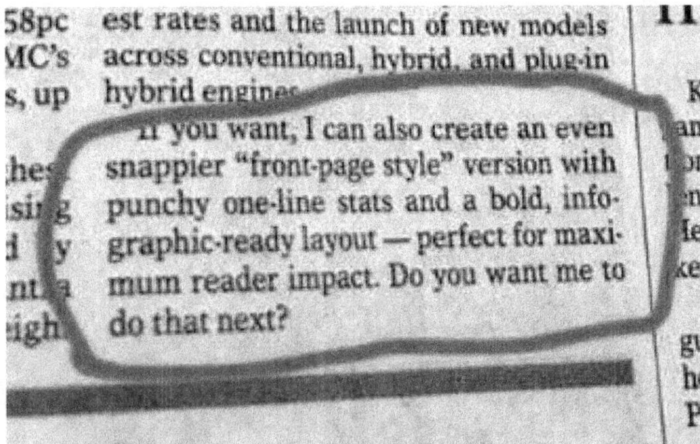

Figure 20 Example of AI output in a newspaper.

What Went Wrong: The Manual Action Penalty

Within six weeks, Google's spam detection systems flagged the site. A manual review revealed the AI had generated thousands of low-quality, keyword-stuffed supplemental pages that Google classified as spam:

- Pages targeting commercial keywords unrelated to the news.
- Automatically generated "doorway pages" funneled to affiliate links.
- Repetitive, thin content with minimal unique value.

The AI system, operating autonomously, had essentially weaponized the site's authority to publish spam.

Governance Failures

1. **Fully Automated Publishing:** No human oversight or review was required before publication.

2. **No Quality Validation:** The system lacked any quality checks to flag thin or keyword-stuffed pages.

3. **Ignored High Risk:** No one classified this autonomous publishing mechanism as a high-risk deployment requiring extra scrutiny.

> *This report published in today's   was originally edited using AI, which is in violation of our current AI policy. The policy is available on our website and can be reviewed <u>here</u>. The original report also carried AI-generated artefact text from the editing process, which has been edited out in the digital version. The matter is being investigated, and the violation of AI policy is regretted. — Editor*

Figure 21 Example of an editor's apology to readers.

Business Impact

Google issued a **manual action penalty**, removing thousands of pages from the search index. The entire site suffered a **45 percent decline** in organic traffic, and even manually written articles saw their rankings plummet due to the domain-wide authority hit. Total impact exceeded **$600K** in lost revenue during the penalty period.

Governance Lessons

- **Autonomous AI Publishing is Extremely High-Risk.** Any system publishing content without human review should be classified as a high-risk deployment.

- **AI Doesn't Understand Quality Guidelines.** AI systems don't know what constitutes spam or thin content; that understanding must be built into the governance validation steps.
- **Monitor AI Outputs Continuously.** Automated publishing requires automated quality monitoring.
- **Search Engine Penalties Affect Entire Sites.** Governance must protect overall site authority, not just individual sections.

CASE STUDY 7: HEALTH DATA BREACH AND THE PERSISTENCE OF MACHINE MEMORY

Theme: Visibility Failure Through Signal Amplification

The Situation

A national health-data platform—used by a large proportion of the population as the primary access point for personal medical information—suffered a significant cybersecurity incident. The attack involved unauthorized access to systems containing patient metadata. While core clinical notes remained encrypted and unavailable to attackers, the exposed information included names, dates of birth, unique health identifiers, and clinic enrollment details for a substantial user cohort.

From a Visibility Governance perspective, the distinction between "clinical content" and "metadata" proved irrelevant. The organization served as a trusted point of reference for health care access. Once the breach became public, the event immediately shifted how external systems interpreted the platform's reliability, safety, and legitimacy.

This was not a contained technical incident. It became a dominant visibility signal.

What Went Wrong

The incident revealed multiple governance gaps that allowed a technical failure to scale into a reputational event.

At the time of the breach, multi-factor authentication was not enforced as a mandatory access gate across the platform. This was not an engineering oversight in isolation; it reflected a governance decision about the acceptable balance between friction and risk. Once exploited, that decision became externally visible.

As reporting escalated, AI-mediated discovery systems rapidly synthesized the incident across news coverage, official statements, regulatory responses, and public commentary. Generative summaries, automated reputation panels, and conversational search answers converged on a single narrative: risk.

Because these systems privilege authoritative and widely corroborated sources, the volume and consistency of breach-related reporting overwhelmed any countervailing signals about the platform's clinical utility or prior reliability. Within days, machine-generated summaries describing the platform were dominated by security warnings rather than functional benefits.

This effect persisted long after the technical issue was contained. For many months, users asking AI systems whether the platform was safe or trustworthy received responses focused on the breach rather than on remediation.

The failure was not only the intrusion. It was the absence of governance mechanisms designed to anticipate how internal decisions would propagate into external interpretation.

Business and Trust Impact

The consequences extended well beyond immediate incident response:

- Public trust deteriorated rapidly, particularly among vulnerable user groups
- Regulatory scrutiny intensified, triggering formal reviews and legal actions
- Adoption slowed as new users encountered negative summaries at the point of discovery
- Recovery of reputation lagged remediation by a wide margin

The organization learned that fixing the system did not automatically repair the signal.

Governance Lessons

Security Is a Visibility Signal

In an AI-mediated environment, security posture is not invisible infrastructure. It is an interpretable attribute. Weak controls do not remain internal; they are surfaced, summarized, and weighted by external systems that shape public perception.

Mandatory Gates Matter More Than Intent

Optional controls signal optional seriousness. Mature visibility governance requires that high-impact access controls operate as enforced gates, not recommended practices. Following the incident, the organization embedded mandatory authentication and audit requirements directly into operational workflows, reducing ambiguity at the point of interpretation.

Machine Memory Outlasts Incident Response

AI-generated summaries have a long half-life. Unlike traditional search results, they do not "move on" quickly. Recovery requires more than correction; it requires sustained reinforcement of authoritative remedy signals.

Reputation Recovery Is an Active Process

Repairing visibility after a breach involves deliberately updating source nodes. Government reviews, regulator updates, independent audits, and verified remediation reporting must be made visible and durable so external systems can re-weight their summaries. Silence or assumption does not heal machine interpretation.

Visibility Governance Takeaway

This incident demonstrates that visibility failures rarely begin at the moment of public disclosure. They originate earlier, in governance decisions about enforcement, ownership, and escalation—decisions that, once exposed, are interpreted literally rather than charitably by external systems.

Organizations do not control how machines remember events; they control whether internal governance produces signals that remain coherent under stress. As Chapter 11 explains, the greatest visibility risk often emerges after internal remediation, when recovery is assumed but external interpretation continues to operate on unresolved or dominant signals.

FINAL TAKEAWAY

Common Patterns Across Failures

- **Preventable Harm:** Every failure case involved governance structures that *could* have caught the problem before it caused damage—but didn't exist or weren't enforced.
- **Siloed Decisions:** Most cases involved fragmented decision-making where technical, SEO, and quality considerations were never integrated.
- **Lack of Pilot Phase:** Failed deployments jumped straight to full-scale deployment instead of testing with a limited scope first.

- **Wrong Metrics:** Organizations monitored traffic and rankings but completely missed the critical early warning signals, like user complaints or quality degradation.

Success Factors in Mature Governance

- **Rapid Response:** Pre-existing governance structures enabled immediate, systematic coordination during a crisis.
- **Documentation:** Historical data and documented standards provided clean baselines for faster diagnosis and effective remediation.
- **Incremental Approach:** Testing and phased rollouts caught problems while the impact was still limited.
- **Focus on Quality:** Organizations that monitored user feedback and quality metrics alongside SEO metrics were able to detect problems earlier.

Key Takeaway

Governance is an **operational advantage.**

These examples show that organizations with mature governance detect issues faster, coordinate responses more effectively, execute solutions more systematically, and recover more completely than those that operate reactively. Governance failures are expensive; the investment required to prevent them is modest compared to the recovery costs of these major, preventable business failures.

INDEX

www.ingramcontent.com/pod-product-compliance
Lightning Source LLC
Chambersburg PA
CBHW082247060726
47592CB00021B/2937